THE HARDWORKING HOME

Inspiring | Educating | Creating | Entertaining

Brimming with creative inspiration, how-to projects, and useful information to enrich your everyday life, Quarto Knows is a favorite destination for those pursuing their interests and passions. Visit our site and dig deeper with our books into your area of interest: Quarto Creates, Quarto Cooks, Quarto Homes, Quarto Lives, Quarto Drives, Quarto Explores, Quarto Gifts, or Quarto Kids.

26 25 24 23 22   1 2 3 4 5

ISBN: 978-0-7603-7277-7

Digital edition published in 2022
eISBN: 978-0-7603-7278-4

Library of Congress Cataloging-in-Publication Data available
Cover Image: Ashley McLeod
Page Layout: *tabula rasa* graphic design

Printed in China

Black & Decker The Hardworking Home

Created by: The Editors of Cool Springs Press, in cooperation with BLACK+DECKER.

NOTICE TO READERS

For safety, use caution, care, and good judgment when following the procedures described in this book. The publisher and BLACK+DECKER cannot assume responsibility for any damage to property or injury to persons as a result of misuse of the information provided.

The techniques shown in this book are general techniques for various applications. In some instances, additional techniques not shown in this book may be required. Always follow manufacturers' instructions included with products, since deviating from the directions may void warranties. The projects in this book vary widely as to skill levels required: some may not be appropriate for all do-it-yourselfers, and some may require professional help.

Consult your local building department for information on building permits, codes, and other laws as they apply to your project.

BLACK+DECKER ™

THE HARDWORKING HOME

A DIY Guide to Working, Learning, and Living at Home

Mark Johanson

COOL
SPRINGS
PRESS

Contents The Hardworking Home

Introduction

The movement toward living remotely and self-sufficiently was growing steadily long before the coronavirus lit a bonfire beneath it. Even as those flames die down, it is clear that we are now confronting what is so often described as a "new normal." The entire dynamic of social interaction has been permanently altered and the fallout is here to stay. The bottom line is that as we proceed into the future, we will be spending more time in our houses, condos, and apartments, and the impulse has never been stronger to make our spaces more comfortable, flexible, and hard working for everyone who lives, learns, and works there.

From home offices to home schooling to home entertainment, today's households have necessarily become functional microcosms of society. Before the pandemic, somewhere between 5 and 20 percent of full-time employees worked remotely from home. At the height of the outbreak, more than half did. And, even as the dust settles, it is estimated that at least a quarter of us will be performing our jobs from offices in our homes. Distance learning also will endure as an important educational tool. While we ease back into less restrictive social distancing guidelines, it nevertheless makes sense to create a fun, vibrant atmosphere for entertaining ourselves and our guests within the safe confines of our homes. The goal, in short, is to improve your environment so you do not become someone who says, "I don't work from home; I live at work."

BLACK+DECKER The Hardworking Home is fundamentally a project book that presents a wide range of achievable home improvements to help you upgrade (and work with) your home to better meet our shifting world. Some of the projects are quite simple and others require a little more DIY experience. But the overriding commonality is that they are curated with the forward-looking filter of making our lives better, more efficient, and more satisfying in the new world landscape. Tips, hints, hacks, and full-blown DIY projects; these are hardworking improvements meant to last. So, take your time and take care when you work—it looks like this will be a long ride.

A bit of remodeling can go a long way if you want to expand your usable living space without adding onto your house.

What Makes a Hardworking Home?

All homes are hardworking, of course. Shelter, warmth, a place to cook and eat, bathrooms, and spots for relaxation: the list of valuable contributions of any house is long. Plus, they are where we keep our stuff. But most houses can work harder if the homeowner uses some creativity and determination. Even a 5,000-square-foot mini-mansion can be made more efficient and gain functionality with some planning. Why does it matter? Because now, more than any time in recent history, our homes are the engines of our economy, if not the locales that support how we make our livings. Like any business, we find ourselves scrambling for ways to make our living spaces ever more efficient and profitable.

A hardworking home is one that has been put under a microscope and evaluated with a strong dose of reality and practicality. Is every room in your house pulling its weight? Or are there some slackers that you've become accustomed to when, if you examine the room closely, you'll have to admit that the space is being underused if not wasted? If, for example, you have a dedicated gift-wrapping room, you really need to think about your priorities and utilization (unless gift-wrapping is your business).

The journey to a more productive home begins with a clear-eyed evaluation: a room-by-room examination of how you use each area counterposed with what you want your home to provide.

As far as usage, the home office is an increasingly necessary starting point, but your home potentially can support your lifestyle in many other ways: a craft area where you can pursue your avocation in peace and make a big mess in the process; a place for the kids to hang out and study; personal space or the rec room of your dreams; more storage; a home theater; a mother-in-law apartment; or a welcoming guest room. The only limit to your list is your imagination. Helping you transform underused space into something functional is the main objective of this book. And perhaps the best news is that you'll learn to do the necessary work yourself.

Wear appropriate clothing and safety gear.

Personal safety is perhaps the most critical element of any home improvement project. Here are some safety considerations to keep in mind.

- Know your tools and their safety features, including blade guards and dust collection bags.

- Keep the work environment clean and neat. Get rid of debris and packaging right away.

- Be sure to have adequate ventilation, especially when working with paints, adhesives, and solvents.

- Control dust through ventilation and by masking off the work area from the rest of the house when possible.

- Keep a well-stocked first aid kit close at hand, as well as a telephone for making emergency calls.

- Do not use power tools in wet or damp conditions.

- If the electrical circuits you are using do not have ground-fault (GFCI) protection, use an extension cord that has a GFCI adapter.

- Always wear sensible clothing with long sleeves and pants that don't fit too loosely. Wear safety apparel, including eye protection, work gloves, and ear protection.

Planning and Preparation

Any project you undertake will benefit from research, careful thought, and good planning. This is especially true when your plan involves making changes, both structural and nonstructural, to your house. Your ideas and goals need to make sense and conform to home standards and codes, and your implementation should follow logical steps that keep you on schedule and budget.

Even if you own your home, there are definite dos and don'ts to be aware of as you work out how to put your ideas into effect. Structural changes or working on wiring or plumbing likely will require a building permit from your local building department. To obtain this, you will need to submit a plan and/or plan drawing that conforms to the building codes in force in your municipality. You'll also need to pay a fee, usually based on the value of the remodeling work. And some, but not all, permits require on-site inspections and approval at key points in the project. The best strategy is to involve your building department from the start. Tell them what you are planning and ask which codes are important to be aware of as you go. Most inspectors appreciate the effort as getting things right from the start makes their job easier, too.

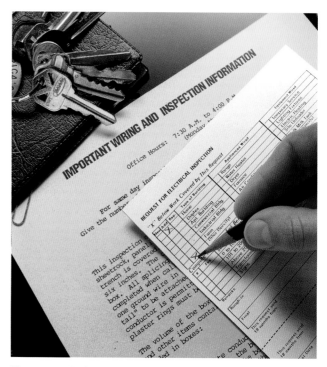

The peace of mind from knowing your projects resulted in a safe home that won't fail an inspection is worth the hassle of following codes and obtaining permits.

7 ft.
6 in.
min.

5 ft.
min.

50 sq. ft. floor space
for kitchens min.

6 ft.
8 in.
min

6 ft.
4 in.
min.

Unfinished
basement

Critical Room Dimensions and Requirements

The rooms in your house are not interchangeable. If you are considering adding or changing functions for any room, be aware of some of the following room dimension requirements.

- A habitable room should not have any wall that is less than 7 feet long.

- Ceiling height should be at least 7 feet, 6 inches for all rooms, including hallways, bathrooms, laundry rooms, and basements.

- Beams, ductwork, and other obstructions may extend up to 6 inches below the minimum ceiling height as long as they are spaced at least 4 feet apart.

- Habitable rooms cannot have more than half of their floor area located beneath a ceiling that slopes and is shorter than 7 feet, 6 inches, such as in dormers and kneewall areas.

- A habitable room can be as small as 70 square feet but no smaller, as long as at least one room in the home is larger than 120 square feet. Specialty rooms that are not used for prolonged occupancy, such as kitchens and bathrooms, may be smaller in floor space.

- A hallway should be at least 3 feet wide.

- Sleeping rooms and habitable basements must have at least one egress (escape) window or door. An egress window should have a clear opening at least 5 $7/10$ square feet in dimension, with a minimum height of 24 inches and minimum width of 20 inches (see page 51).

- Any screens, bars, or protective covers on emergency exits must be removable from inside the home without requiring the use of tools or keys.

- Exit doors must be at least 3 feet wide and 6 feet, 8 inches tall.

A portable, adjustable shelving system quickly converts a quiet corner into semi-private office space (see page 46).

Section 1:
Adapting Space

Upgrading your house into a hardworking home is mostly a matter of good decisions and creative solutions. Whether your goal is to carve out an efficient home office, set up a productive study area for home learning, or create more living space to support a variety of activities, the answer is either to adapt what you have or commit to remodeling.

Section 2 (page 31) covers DIY home remodeling in the form of such things as building a wall, adding lighting, or installing a dropdown ceiling. This section focuses on simpler changes, such as rearranging what you have or adding a new piece or two to make your existing space more pleasant and functional without wholesale changes and a lot of work. You can easily reverse any changes presented here if you no longer need the adaptation.

This section includes:

- Tips and Solutions for Any Room

- Adapting Dining Rooms

- Adapting Kitchens

- Adapting Family Rooms

- Adapting Bedrooms

Adapting space for expanded functionality can take many forms. Create a temporary standing desk with an ironing board. Too short? A pair of yoga blocks can give it lift. Ingenuity, labor, and remedies—both ad hoc and long-term—make a hardworking home work for you.

Most experts agree we will continue to incorporate the lessons about learning and working at a distance into our homes.

Tips and Solutions for Any Room

Creative choices can save you time, money, and work when creating a home office. Every situation is different, but the need for dedicated, at-home workspace is universal. Whether you live in a home with multiple rooms, a garage, and a basement or in an apartment or condo with more limited space, you can employ your creativity to establish your own hardworking home.

A wood frame with infill strips is an effective way to divide space but maintain an airy quality.

Cabinets and countertops nestled into the corner of this basement office become file cabinets and workspace without taking over the room.

Corners are not the only option for creating a home office or study area.

Home Office Décor

How you decorate your home office, exercise area, entertaining area, or any room, really, impacts your productivity and enjoyment of the space. The principal elements of home décor are color, equipment/furniture, and artwork.

There are few better or cheaper ways to utterly transform an existing room than to give it a new coat of paint. The question is: which color to use? Bearing in mind that a home office is an integral part of your overall living space, it makes sense to consider your current color scheme, especially if the workspace is not set apart by a distinct border, such as a door.

You can spend a lot of time delving into the depths of color theory and speculating on which colors have what impact, such as productivity versus relaxation. It may ring of pop psychology at times, but those who study the question of color tend to highlight the positive effects of three colors: blue, green, and yellow.

A lighter shade of blue that moves toward teal or blue/gray is a popular home office color that some find relaxing without making them drowsy. Green is regarded as energizing and motivational. Yellow, some say, can spur creativity. While, pure white evokes a clinical feeling in many; tempered to off-white, it can feel more welcoming. Reds are thought to inspire immediate action, which can be a benefit but can also work against activities that demand a more reasoned approach.

Whichever color scheme you choose, the one piece of advice most experts seem to agree upon is to use that color with some discretion. You don't have to paint every wall in your chosen tone, and often selecting a contrasting trim color can preserve the beneficial aspects but keep the color from becoming overwhelming. Plus, a separate wall color will set off a work area and indicate the change in function.

A home workspace should reflect the preferences of the user, but not to the point that it becomes a distraction.

A medium- to light-toned blue with a little green or gray is said to have a calming effect, a nice counterpoint to the splashes of bold accent colors in this kid's room and work area.

Bold colors are fun and promote creativity no matter your age. Yellow, whether bright or muted, is thought to promote creative exploration.

A pleasant green creates an energetic response, amplified by a few green elements, particularly houseplants.

Light

The basic strategies for effective home office lighting change little from room to room. Later chapters discuss specific lighting requirements in greater detail as it applies to the topic at hand. Set up your work area so the light falls across it, not directly from behind or in your eyes as you work. Manipulate artificial light with swiveling floor lamps or desk lamps to supplement overhead and natural lighting. The tips here apply no matter if you are setting up a workspace in a bright second bedroom or a windowless room in the basement.

- Use multiple light sources, including natural light, ambient light that illuminates the entire room, and directed task lighting, usually in the form of wall lamps or desk lamps. Unless you are enlarging or adding a window or installing a skylight (great DIY projects), there is not much you can do to alter the amount and quality of available natural light in your room. You can replace room-darkening shades or blinds or perhaps trim back outdoor foliage that may be blocking light entry, but basically, you've got what you've got. You can relocate overhead light spots that create less glare and fewer shadows in your work area (another great DIY project; see page 34), but you can also manage the intensity of the light by switching to different bulbs, such as natural-light LED, or by adding or replacing a light diffuser.

- Beware of shadows and glare. Orient your workspace so the overhead light, if you have one, is not directly behind you, which will create glare on your computer screen. Position lamps to direct light across your workspace and toward your dominant hand to minimize shadows when you write or use your keyboard or mouse.

- Take advantage of the decorating possibilities offered by lamps and lighting. There is a style to match any decorating scheme, from traditional to modern/industrial.

Natural light is free and a wonderful gift from the universe. Supplement it with carefully directed artificial light.

There is no better ventilation than an open window or door, so take advantage when you can and supplement it with mechanical ventilation to improve airflow.

Ventilation

If you are spending the better part of a workday at a workstation in your home, you will appreciate good airflow. As with natural light, there is really no substitute for natural ventilation. To be able to throw open a window on a beautiful spring day is one of the greatest benefits of working from home. Realistically, you'll probably need to make some improvements to your hardworking room, whether you are using it as an office or a recreation/exercise area.

Vent fans in the window, through a wall, or mounted on the ceiling are mechanical ways to improve airflow. You can even have a whole-house ventilation system installed. Later chapters pertaining to historically ventilation-challenged rooms, such as basements and garages, discuss these options. Without making major home improvements, here are a few tips for improving ventilation.

- If your room has a window air conditioner, run it even without the cooling function to improve air circulation.

- Point fans in or out? This question has raged for generations: is it better to enjoy the immediate relief of a cool breeze on your warm skin or should you direct a box fan in a window outdoors to "blow the warm air out?" The debate has not been resolved, but you can skip the question entirely by installing a two-fan unit in the window, with one fan directed outward and the other blowing inside the room.

- Add a dehumidifier. This is less for ventilation issues than air quality, but anything that improves the air you are breathing and keeps it moving is worth doing.

Noise

Sound control is important in any working environment, but it is especially challenging in the home, where the activities of other family members—including pets—can intrude. Many remodeling projects, such as adding a second layer of drywall or a layer of mass-loaded vinyl, can help control noise. Metal channels placed between the drywall and the wall studs also reduce vibration, which intensifies sound transfer. But for immediate, temporary soundproofing, there are a few options you can employ without cutting into your walls, floors, or ceilings.

- Add carpeting or an area rug with a pad if the room has hard floorcoverings, such as wood or tile.

- Hang large paintings or textile art on the walls.

- Add a door. If there is already a door, add an exterior-style door sweep to cover the gap at the bottom.

- Add acoustic tile panels to the walls, doors, ceiling, or all of the above.

- Keep outdoor noise out by improving caulking and weatherstripping around the windows or by upgrading to double-paned, insulated window units.

Self-adhesive foam soundproofing panels bonded to the walls, ceiling, or both make a big impact on noise control. The type shown here is commonly used in recording studios to dampen sound transfer.

Hanging heavy textiles or affixing acoustical tile to key noise transfer points, such as hollow-core doors, can reduce noise transfer. Solid doors offer a more permanent improvement.

A sturdy worksurface, a comfortable desk chair, convenient storage, and a comfortable break spot can turn just about any space into a pleasant and functional home office.

Furnishings

How should you furnish your new home office or other home work area? No one knows better than you. Take an honest accounting of which furnishings you actually used on a daily basis in your previous office space. A large file cabinet is an absolute necessity in some lines of work, but for others it quickly becomes a storage vault of forgotten papers to recycle. Challenge your preconceptions when it comes to your needs. With a little modification, a floor-to-ceiling bookcase, for instance, can do double-duty as a home office. Add base cabinets or matching dressers, install a countertop that spans the bases or dressers, and then add the bookshelves on top of the counter.

Regardless of the secondary and more task-oriented features, just about any home office starts with a desk. Do you require a large worksurface on which you can spread work out or do you only need a sturdy place to set your laptop? Will your desk be a fixture of meeting with clients or will a kitchen or dining room table suffice? Here are a few more desk considerations:

- Consider a sit-to-stand desk. You can set these adjustable furnishings to a normal seated height—usually 30 to 32 inches—or raise them if you want to stretch out a bit and stand while you work (a recommended practice if you can handle it physically).

- If you are using a computer with a peripheral keyboard, look into a pull-out keyboard tray to conserve desktop space.

- Shop around. You'll find plenty of traditional desks in many sizes and configurations. But you'll also find desks with more economical footprints, such as corner or fold-up desks, or perhaps even one that "floats" on mounting hardware attached to the wall, keeping the leg space completely clear.

- Look for a comfortable chair with good lumbar support. Many people prefer a chair that swivels or reclines, as long as it maintains enough rigidity and support. And, even in a small office space, wheels can be a big plus.

Dining and Living Rooms

The dining room and living room are the first spots many people look when they are seeking to boost the work output of a home or apartment. This is mostly because these are typically the most underused rooms in the home. Plus, they likely have some of the key elements you need already in place, such as a table, cabinets, and shelving.

In a dining room:

- Use existing furniture, such as china cabinets and buffets, to store office supplies.

- Buy a rolling utility cart or rolling drawers so you can easily remove your office supplies when you are eating or entertaining.

An extra-tall bay or two in front of the open area makes space for a computer and peripherals, such as this printer, and it all looks right at home in a dining room or living room.

Get in the habit of packing away work when it's time to use a dining room table for other purposes.

Place an unassuming DIY worksurface supported by sawhorses against the wall anywhere in a casual living room and use it as a snack center or buffet for hosting.

Even the few inches added by a computer stand can make it more comfortable for an adult to work at a dining table or desk, which tend to be only 29 to 30 inches tall.

Keep things on the level. These two workspaces rely on matching dressers and sturdy end panels for their support and storage of supplies for both work and entertaining.

- Deal with cords by adding a closer electrical outlet and/or using cable organizers.

- Dedicate a tablecloth to protect the dining table surface while you work.

- Mount a multi-outlet electrical strip to the underside of the table or even consider installing a grommet with a pop-up outlet in the tabletop.

In a living room:

- The best strategy for adding work functionality is to keep the desk and related furnishings as far out of the way as you can. This is generally pretty easy to do.

- Consider rearranging your furniture so you can slide a desk up to the back of a sofa ala a sofa table. This effect works best if the desk is taller than the sofa.

- If your living room has a coat closet, consider replacing it with a coat rack and converting the closet to an office (see page 82).

Kitchens

The kitchen is a natural spot for a workstation, if only because you are likely using the kitchen that way already for paying bills or helping a kid with homework. There are plenty of tricks you can use to keep your office equipment out of the way, while also protecting it from normal kitchen splatter:

- Store a wireless printer inside a cabinet. Add a shelf with drawer slides so you can simply pull out the printer when you need it.

- Use a tambour-type breadbox on the counter to store office or crafting supplies.

- Keep the new workspace as far from the stove and sink as possible.

- Add drawers to a kitchen island.

- Mount your computer monitor on the wall to conserve desk space.

- Use kitchen-themed storage, such as a wine rack, for storing rolled-up papers or magazines.

- Convert a pantry into a closet office or dedicate a portion of the storage and shelving for office supplies.

- Use existing countertops or your kitchen table for work, but dedicate one cabinet for stashing the work materials when it's time to cook.

Remove a 28- to 30-inch wide (at least) base cabinet but not its countertop to create a built-in desk with chair space and an undercounter keyboard tray.

Partition off the end of a kitchen cabinet run with permanent, full-height walls on each side to define a semi-private work area.

Repurpose kitchen drawers to house office or crafting supplies that support the activities you regularly do in your kitchen space.

Take advantage of an existing nook in a transition area by sliding in a small desk or other furnishing. If you don't have a nook, move a closet wall to open up the area.

Family Rooms

Most family rooms are already hardworking, multi-purpose spaces designed to be well-used. If you still have an active family living at home, this might not be the best room for adding a new home office or crafting area. Without making major remodeling improvements, you'll likely end up in one another's way. But if you find yourself in the position of being an empty nester, or your family room just isn't getting much use, it could be a perfect candidate for adapting to a home office or workspace. Here are some easy tips to retain the functionality of the family room while adding to it.

- Divide the space. A large family room is a great spot for a moveable room divider (see page 118).

- Put things on wheels. A rolling desk and rolling file cabinets can move out of the way to create space for relaxing in front of the TV.

- Look for multi-purpose or convertible furniture.

- Choose activity spaces that lend themselves to the space, such as a home gym with movable equipment or a crafting table and supply storage.

Take advantage of the WIFI and electronics support in your built-in entertainment area by adding a desk, workspace, and peripherals.

Choose an unobtrusive desk, such as this glass one, if you are plopping it into a corner of the busy room.

A family room adapts easily to a home gym, as long as you can easily store the exercise equipment when it's not in use. Enjoy the entertainment options as you work out.

Bedrooms

An unused bedroom is the first place most of us turn to when the need for a home office arises, but not everyone has this option. Nevertheless, even an occupied bedroom can provide space for a desk and some minimal storage without compromising the room's primary functionality.

In a bedroom, perhaps more than in any other room, it is very important to take measures to separate the sleeping space from the workspace. It's a practical issue, but also a quality of life one that you can accomplish with room dividers or even curtains. Or, you can do it by following some simple tips.

- Position your desk so your back faces the bed when you are at work. Out of sight out of mind.

- Add separate lighting for the work area, even if it is only a desk lamp. You should be able to turn off your work light at the end of the day without being left in the dark.

- If space is an issue, consider down-sizing your bed.

- Look into convertible beds, such as futons, sofa beds, or murphy beds, to free up space.

- Upgrade the ventilation. A ceiling fan is good for sleeping or for working and, positioned in the right place, it can visually separate the room.

- Look into buying a corner desk.

- If you will be having video conferences from your home office, make sure your computer camera views an appropriate background.

Create visual separation with different paint colors or shades. Split space in a dresser between typical contents and work supplies.

A partial, bump-out kneewall attached to a bedroom wall defines a work area and a cozy nook for the bed. It also makes a useful horizontal surface for storage and display. With the same wall color and base trim treatment, the wall blends nicely into the room.

This two-kid setup is almost completely symmetrical, which any parent knows is important. It also includes useful pegboard hangers (see page 164), two corkboards, and a shared set of drawers that tuck underneath a plain worktable. A freestanding privacy divider set upon the desktop can further divvy up the space.

Most kids love a loft bed, and parents love the loft's efficiency. Use the space below as a work or storage area.

Customize lighting and add soundproofing or upgraded electrical/data service to create a comfortable, efficient home office.

Section 2:
Creating Space

As much as we'd like to be able to snap our fingers and suddenly have more living space, it doesn't work that way. But the good news is that the space we crave may already be there. It only takes some imagination and work to repurpose an unused or underused area in your home into a high-functioning room for working or relaxing. A spare bedroom, the basement, the garage, or even an attic can be creatively converted into new and well-used space in your home.

While repurposing a room will likely require some concessions, the first step is to look critically at your priorities and how you currently use the space. How often does your guest room have guests? Can you clear basement or attic clutter and efficiently store those items that make the cut? Compare what you'll lose to what you want to gain. The projects in this section can make little-used space livable.

- Renovating a spare room
- Creating an office or "recess area" in your basement
- How to convert a closet into a home office or study area
- How to renovate a garage and make it comfortable for occupation
- How to convert a shed or outbuilding into an office or craft room

Renovating a Spare Room

If you are lucky, or perhaps simply an empty nester, your house may have a spare room. All you really need is a desk and chair to get started. But making a few fairly minor upgrades will boost the comfort level in the room and help it operate more efficiently.

A home office or workstation has different ergonomic requirements than a bedroom. Depending on how you use the space, a single 15-amp circuit (common in bedrooms) may not have the power or the number of outlets that you need. While a fresh coat of paint might be a good starting point for converting the room, take a look at making a few upgrades to the wiring and lighting.

An empty bedroom is a blank canvas. An overhead light and a window are a good start, but consider adding accent and task lighting, and perhaps a few outlets, as well.

You can modify even a small spare room through lighting and surface improvements, as well as furnishings, to be more comfortable and effective for one or more learners.

Lighting Improvements

There is virtually no limit to the variety of desk and floor lamps you can find that can provide directed task lighting while minimizing glare and shadows (depending on how you place them). Making an upgrade or two to the permanent room lighting makes sense no matter how you intend to use the room. Track lighting and recessed lighting are two good options. In addition to being reliable light sources, they also have an "officey" feel that will make your workspace seem less like a bedroom and more like a hardworking space for getting things done.

A hanging light fixture causes less glare and shadow than lights mounted directly on the ceiling. Some have adjustable height, and shades or diffusers can soften and redirect the light.

HOW MUCH LIGHT DO YOU NEED?

While there are mathematical ratios and algorithms for calculating the minimum amount of light or brightness (different measures) any room requires, they are difficult if not headspinning to apply. This is not just because every room has different wall colors, natural light, and a different function; it is because the number of available light source types has expanded and they are not always easy to compare. But if you want to take a stab at running the algorithm to calculate how much light you should have in your newly repurposed room, here are some basics.

The two new vocabulary words you'll need to learn are *lumens* and *footcandles*. A lumen is the measure of how much visible brightness is generated by a light source in a set period of time. For example, a 100-watt incandescent bulb generates around 1,500 lumens. This is roughly equivalent to the number of lumens emitted by a 16-watt LED bulb. You can find online calculators that ask you to input the square footage of the room to calculate the minimum amount of light it requires, expressed in lumens. For example, a 10 x 10-foot bedroom with 8-foot ceilings requires total illumination of 1,500 lumens (16 or 18 LED watts). A home office of the same dimension demands 6,000 lumens (75 LED watts). By adding up the total lumen output of the existing and planned light sources, you can determine if your remodel meets the minimum

requirements. And obviously, a bedroom that is transformed to an office will need a lighting boost.

It doesn't end there. Footcandles measure how bright the light from a source appears to the eye when viewed from one foot away. This is significant in that various types of light sources have differing footcandle output so, for example, 1,500 lumens of incandescent or fluorescent light will appear dimmer to your eye than 1,500 lumens of LED light (LED is at the top of the footcandle chart for residential lighting). If you really want to get into the weeds, you can investigate the ideal measure of footcandles of light relative to the purpose of your room. Be aware that this can be a difficult calculus. Where most lightbulb packages express lumens, wattage, and projected lifespan, they normally do not mention footcandles, so you'll have to do some research. But just as a relative standard, here are the suggested number of footcandles of light considered ideal for certain rooms by function:

- Living room: 20 footcandles
- Kitchen: 40 footcandles (more in work areas)
- Dining room: 30 footcandles (preferably dimmable)
- Office: 60 to 75 footcandles
- Bedroom: 20 footcandles
- Bathroom: 80 footcandles

A series of canister lights wired together can provide excellent task light in a work area, as well as overhead light.

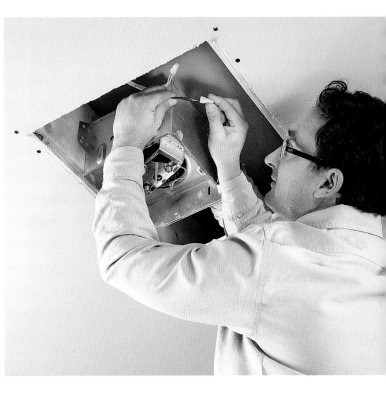

You can install retrofit canister lights from below in a finished ceiling as long as you are able to get the necessary wiring to the location.

LED canister lights, usually spotlights, have become very common and inexpensive. Their efficiency and minimal heat production are assets in a recessed installation.

Recessed canister lights can transform a room and allow you to focus primary or secondary lighting right where you need it. These lights, often sold in multi-packs, are relatively easy to install using mounting bars if you have access from above the ceiling. Otherwise, you can install retrofit models, which rely on spring clamps, from beneath a finished ceiling that does not have overhead access.

Combine a vent fan's environmental improvement contribution with overhead lighting and some appealing style by installing a combination vent fan/ceiling light.

Surface-Mounted Raceway

Converting a spare room—especially a bedroom—for use as a home office, study area, or craft room usually will demand higher performance from the existing room wiring. This is in terms of both power consumption and availability. If you are feeling very ambitious, you can remove all or some of the wall surfaces and add a new electrical circuit and additional outlets. This can make sense if you plan to use the new room heavily and for a long time. But if your goal is to increase the number and location of receptacles so the room doesn't become a rat's nest of extension cords and plug-in strips, there is an easier solution: surface-mounted raceway.

Raceway can mean many things: attaching metal conduit to a basement or garage wall, fastening plastic channels to any wall to organize computer cables, or running wall-mounted metal tracks from existing electrical boxes to supply new wall-mounted outlets on the same circuit. Most building centers carry raceway products, including lengths of metal track to connect wires together with various fittings and boxes to create a protected pathway that extends wires from a live receptacle or switch to brand new outlets.

Before

Install surface-mounted raceway on the walls to expand the utility and convenience of any room with new outlets and circuits.

After

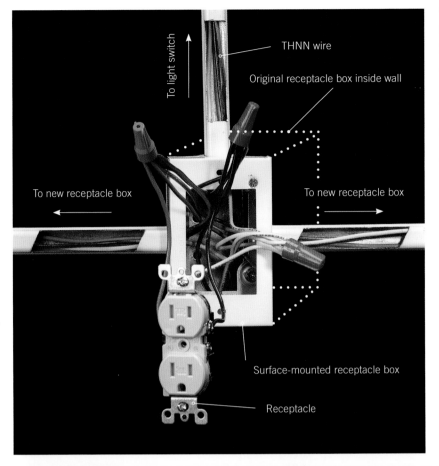

To light switch

THNN wire

Original receptacle box inside wall

To new receptacle box

To new receptacle box

Surface-mounted receptacle box

Receptacle

The receptacle box used to originate a new circuit mounts directly to an existing electrical box in a wall. It contains knockouts into which the raceway tracks fit to carry wire from the receptacle to a new outlet, which is surface-mounted in its new location. Mount the original receptacle on the surface-mounted box and cover it with a coverplate or cover the new receptacle box with a coverplate if the old receptacle was not getting regular use.

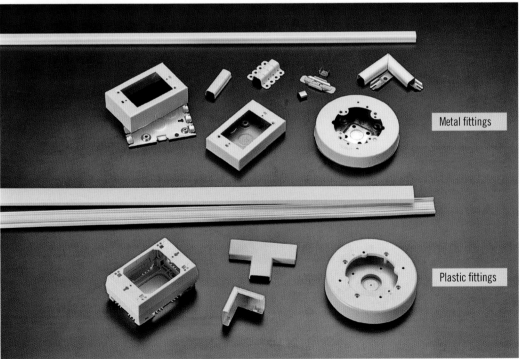

Metal fittings

Plastic fittings

The two most common surface-mounted raceway systems are made with two-part plastic channels and fittings or metal channel and fittings. Use plastic systems primarily for guiding computer cables and metal component systems if the task is to house electrical wiring. Typical fittings include receptacle and switch boxes with mounting plates; elbow and T-fittings for changing direction of the nonflexible tracks; various clips and fasteners to attach the tracks and boxes; and round, ceiling-mounted boxes for attaching light fixtures.

How to Install Metal Surface-Mounted Raceway

Because of the way the components of a metal raceway system fit together, the best way to install the parts is linearly: start at the origin and add track and fittings until you reach the destination.

1. Shut off the power to the relevant circuit.

2. Remove the coverplate of the receptacle, pull out the device, and disconnect the wiring.

3. Cap off the wires.

4. Attach a mounting plate for the surface-mounted box to the existing receptacle box, threading the capped wires through the access hole in the plate (Photo A).

Choose which knockout on the new receptacle box makes sense for your layout. For example, if you are running raceway to a new outlet elsewhere in the same room, plan on running raceway down from the box and then using an elbow fitting to redirect the track so it can run just above the baseboard until it reaches the new outlet locale. Then, use another elbow to install track upward onto the wall to the new receptacle. The standard is for the bottom of the box to be 16 inches up from the floor. If you are using the new outlet or outlets to power a workstation, consider installing the new box 36 inches above the floor so it will be just above desk height and much more accessible.

The most common metal raceway systems have two-part channels that fit into elbows and tees you attach directly to the walls. You can't retrofit the metal channel covers onto the elbows and tees if they are already attached to the wall, so you need to assemble the parts before you attach the fittings. Then you slide the track into the adjoining fitting before attaching the elbow or tee to the wall (Photo B).

Remove the existing receptacle, cap all wires, and then attach a new surface-mounted base plate to the existing electrical box.

Fit the elbow base into the track section, insert the section into the box, and then attach the elbow base plate on the wall.

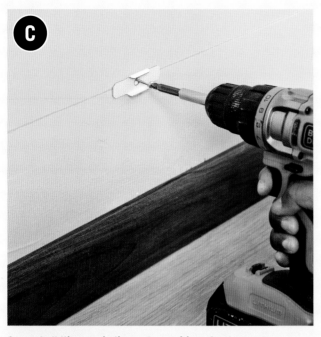

Snap chalkllines to indicate the positions for the track channels, and then attach wall clips into which you'll snap the tracks.

Snap the tracks onto the mounting clips, moving sequentially from start to end.

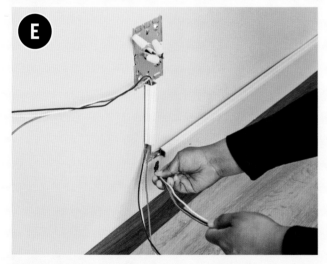

With the tracks but not the elbow and tee covers in place, feed the THNN supply wires through the network from start to destination.

Snap the elbow and tee covers onto their base plates once you have threaded the wires through the tracking channels.

The elbow and tee fittings do most of the work when it comes to securing the raceway to the wall, but longer runs of track should have clips that they fit into to attach to the wall.

5. Use chalklines as a reference to locate the mounting clips for the tracks and attach them to the wall at stud locations or with wall anchors (Photo C).

6. Attach channels to the elbow and tee bases and fill in the channel run but do not attach the elbow and tee covers.

7. Snap the channel covers sequentially onto the bases and clips (Photo D).

8. Attach the base plate for the outlet to the wall, completing the track channel run.

Use THNN individual wires (*not* sheathed cable, such as Romex) to feed the wires from the origination point and to the destination. It helps to wrap the ends of the power, neutral, and ground wires together with electrical tape before threading them into the tracks (Photo E). Once the wire is in place, snap the covers onto the elbow and tee bases (Photo F).

9. Make the new wiring connections at the original box and the new box. Be sure to attach the ground wires to the grounding terminal on the receptacle base plates (Photo G).

10. Screw the receptacles or other devices to their boxes and attach the new box to the base plate (Photo H).

11. Add coverplates, turn the circuit back on, and test.

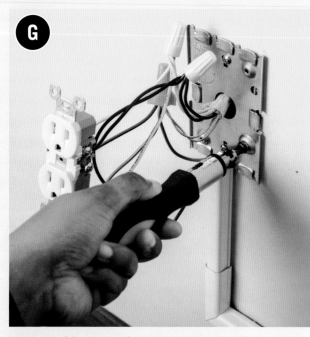

Make the wiring connections to the new receptacle, including screwing the ground wire to the grounding terminal on the receptacle base plate.

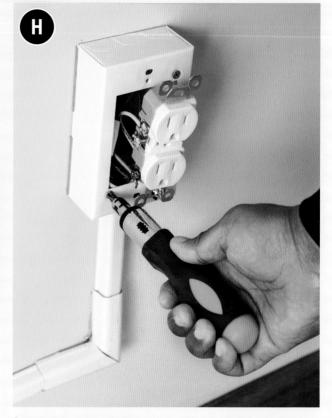

Secure the receptacle box cover to the base plate and then attach the receptacle to the box. Add the coverplate.

If you need to turn a corner or reach a ceiling with raceway, use corner fittings. These look like elbow fittings but are oriented so the base plates are flat against both walls of the corners where a wall meets another wall or a ceiling. Do not snap the corner fitting covers on until you have run the wire through the raceway. Once all of the wiring is run and secured with coverplates, hook up the devices being powered by the new circuit (inset photo).

There are many ways to cut conduit and raceway, including reciprocating saws and chop saws with a bi-metal blade. But for most homeowners working on a modest raceway project, the most controllable way to cut the track and conduit is with an ordinary hacksaw.

Track Lighting

If you want to improve the light in your new office or otherwise repurposed bedroom, track lighting is an easy solution. Not only does it increase illumination while allowing you to direct the light where it is needed, it just simply makes the room feel more like a hardworking room and less like a place to sleep.

You can install track lighting as a one-for-one replacement for a ceiling light or as secondary lighting with a new circuit and separate switching. Alternatively, you can find track light systems that have a plug-in cord to simplify installation.

Stylistically, track lighting heads change often to reflect contemporary design trends. If this is important to you, look to the original manufacturer of your track system for updated head models, as the connecting

Replace a plain ceiling light with a 3- to 12-foot track light system and as many heads as you want to improve overall lighting and allow you to direct lights as needed.

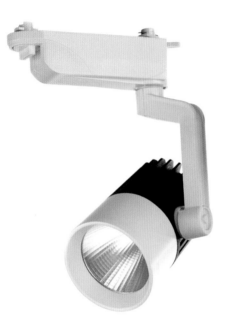

Low-voltage track lights require a transformer that can either be integral to the light head or located at the infeed end of the lighting track. They consume less energy but look bulkier, and the head style options are more limited.

mechanism between lights heads and the track is usually unique to each maker. If you want the lights themselves to blend in, choose white or cream tracks and light heads. To make a design statement, select more modern black or metallic finishes, such as brushed stainless steel. Or, investigate the new options for pendant lights that drop down as much as 40 inches from a clip-in base that mounts in the light track.

One of the benefits of track lighting is that it is highly customizable. You can employ everything from a 24-inch track with a couple of lights to a large U-shaped track that uses 90-degree elbow fittings to make turns and supports many light heads. The number of light heads each track will support depends on the wattage rating of the track. In general, don't use more than one light head per foot of track. If you use LED track light bulbs, you can get away with more light heads, since they draw considerably less wattage than comparable halogen, fluorescent, or incandescent bulbs.

LOW-VOLTAGE VERSUS LINE-VOLTAGE

Track lights come in two basic types: *low voltage* and *line voltage*. Your 120-volt electrical service powers the more common line voltage lights. Low-voltage track systems require a transformer that converts the 120-volt AC power to 12- or 24-volt DC power. Though not big, the transformer, which is usually placed at the start of the light track, is rather visible. Some low-voltage heads include an integral transformer with each head. Low-voltage light systems consume less energy than line voltage ones. The contact points of track lighting are electrified and exposed, so low-voltage systems offer the advantage of a much more absorbable shock, should you accidentally touch the contact areas. Line voltage equipment has a lower initial cost and more style options.

Track lighting is generally a secondary light source that is combined with other lights, including overhead and pendant lights. It allows you to focus spotlights on areas you want to showcase or wherever you need extra illumination.

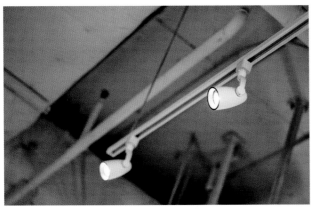

Track light tracks are most often mounted directly to the ceiling to keep the lights as far out of the way as possible. If you have high ceilings or a challenging ceiling structure, you can suspend the tracks to bring the lighting exactly where you want it.

Traditionally, track lighting was designed to be as inconspicuous as possible. Newer products are recognizing the ability of these striking platforms to add style and some modern flair to a room, as with this brushed stainless steel track light with small but stylish light heads.

How to Install Track Lighting

Replacing a plain ceiling light with a track lighting system is a very easy DIY project that can transform an ordinary bedroom into something that feels more hardworking. Because the tracks are surface-mounted, you do not have to cut into the ceiling: a big bonus.

1. Turn off the power at the main service panel.

2. Remove your existing ceiling light to provide access to the electrical box and the feed wires within. Your track light kit should include a mounting strap that is to be attached to the electrical box.

3. Feed the wires through the access hole in the strap and attach the strap to the box (Photo A).

Prepare the track by cutting to length—they are usually sold in 2-, 4-, 6-, and 8-foot sections, so you probably can plan your system so no cutting is necessary. If you are installing an L-shaped or U-shaped track, purchase connector fittings for the track to accommodate your layout (Photo B).

4. Snap the track into the mounting strap and orient it as you plan. Most tracks have predrilled mounting holes. Mark the holes where you need to add fasteners onto the ceiling and remove the track.

5. Drill guide holes at the marked points and use toggle bolts to fasten the track unless the mounting holes happen to line up with ceiling joists, in which case you can simply drive screws (Photo C).

6. With the track secured and the feed wires accessible, attach the power supply fitting for the track system to the feed wires (Photo D). The fitting usually snaps into the track after the wires are connected. Now the track is wired and ready to accept light heads.

7. Snap the cover over the power supply fitting or attach it with screws if your kit is created that way (Photo E). Your kit should have included caps for the ends of the track. Snap these in place now.

8. Insert the light heads into the track by fitting the stems of the heads into the slot and then spinning them so they are perpendicular to the track, which will support them (Photo F).

9. Install all of the heads, set their direction to match your lighting needs, and turn on the power to test.

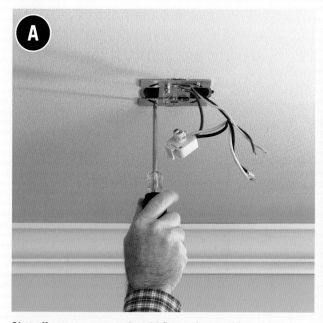

Shut off power, remove the old fixture (or provide a new electrical box with wired hookups), and attach the mounting strap to the electrical box.

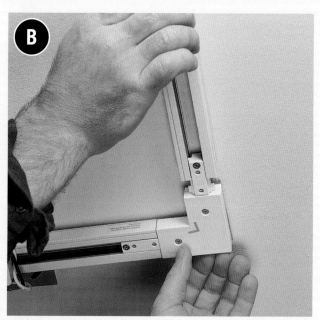

Cut the track section or sections to length as needed and join the sections with connector fittings.

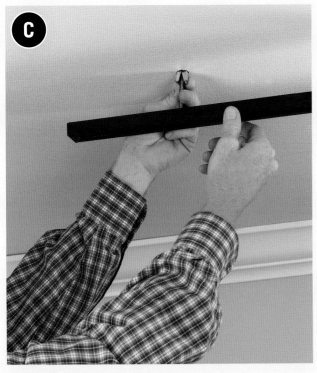

Secure the track to the ceiling using screws where possible and wall anchors, such as toggle bolts, if the predrilled mounting holes do not line up with ceiling joists.

Attach the power supply fitting for the track system to the feed wires and then snap it into the track channel.

Attach the coverplate that conceals the power supply fitting.

Lock the light heads into the track by fitting the stem at the top of each light into the track channel and twisting it to a perpendicular position.

Creating an Office or "Recess Area" in a Basement

If you are fortunate enough to have a full basement, that's likely one of the first places you will look to expand your living space. Be it as a family room, additional bedroom, home office, or an entertainment area (read "bar"), the below-grade area of a house provides promising opportunities. If your basement is already finished, creating new space or a new enclosed room is going to be similar to subdividing any other large room.

If your basement is not already equipped for regular use, there are some things you'll need to address before you start moving into it. The nature of a basement lends itself to low ceiling height, lack of natural lighting, and distracting noise from furnaces, washing machines, and other appliances. You will have to plan around these limits, as there are no practical ways to tackle them. However, you can and should make modifications to control two vital aspects of this below-grade space: humidity and temperature.

Water tends to seep into basements through foundation walls and up through the floor. The typically substandard ventilation used in basements does nothing to mitigate the dampness, and the result can be anything from unpleasant odors to mold and mildew growth. The latter can cause allergic reactions and trigger or aggravate respiratory conditions, sometimes severely. Also, unfinished basements often are not fully integrated into a home's heat plant, in which case new, safe, and reliable heat sources are up to you to install.

However you address the environmental concerns, municipalities enforce a host of building codes that apply to creating habitable rooms in basements (see page 50). Some are specific to basements and others simply apply to basements very commonly.

Basements offer a host of opportunities for remodeling to create a space that can support many activities, including a friendly game of ping pong or pool.

If you can move large furnishings and pieces of equipment into the basement, it can be a great spot for a specialty room, such as an arcade.

If your unfinished basement has plumbing stub-outs, take advantage of them. But always choose a project that you'll use and enjoy.

Creating space is largely about functionality. Carve out a small workstation next to your washer and dryer to make your own quiet getaway when it isn't laundry day.

Is Your Basement Livable?

While a basement may seem like an obvious place to expand the reach of your hardworking home, it is well worth your time to do some evaluation and testing before you get too deep into the process of remodeling it. A few simple tests, some commonsense observations, and a knowledge of what your local building codes allow will give you a clear idea of what you might be up against and what it will take to make the basement environment as pleasant as possible.

An unfinished basement is a blank canvas. Clean and ready to go is ideal, but you can potentially rehab a wet and grimy basement into pleasant living space.

Basement Humidity

Moisture is the number one enemy of basement environments. The cooler temperatures and proximity to ground moisture outside the foundation walls usually means higher humidity levels inside the basement. To measure the humidity, use a hygrometer. You can find this simple device online for ten dollars or less. Take readings in multiple locations in your basement and average them out. The ideal relative humidity in a living space is between 30 and 40 percent. If the readings in your basement are higher than this, you can take action to reduce the levels. The easiest and most obvious is simply to deploy a dehumidifier or two.

A large-capacity dehumidifier will remove 40 or more pints of moisture from the air each day, presuming an air temperature of 65° F and starting humidity level of 60 percent. Medium-capacity models remove 30 to 35 pints of moisture in the same conditions, and generally are less expensive. Small-capacity units draw 20 to 25 pints of water per day from the air, making them better suited for upper-level use. You could also look into a whole-house dehumidifier, which likely would need to be integrated into your house heating/cooling system. They are effective but expensive. Most drain directly into your plumbing drain systems so they do not have tanks that need to be emptied manually, as freestanding models do. For information on physical space improvements you can make to try to address active moisture problems, see page 54.

Hygrometers are inexpensive devices used to determine the humidity level in your basement. Relative humidity between 30% and 40% is ideal.

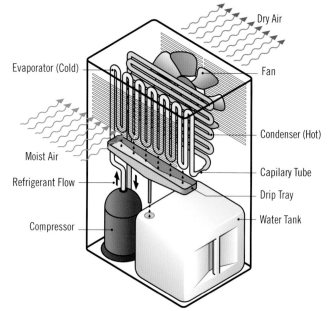

Dry Air

Evaporator (Cold)

Fan

Condenser (Hot)

Moist Air

Capilary Tube

Refrigerant Flow

Drip Tray

Water Tank

Compressor

Dehumidifiers draw air across a series of coils filled with refrigerant to cool the air and cause it to drip condensation into a tank before exhausting the drier air back into the room.

To evaluate whether you have ongoing moisture infiltration problems in your basement, take a couple of simple tests.

To see if moisture is entering your basement through a concrete floor, tape a one-square-foot piece of plastic to the floor. Leave it in place for a day and then check the underside. If there's condensation, it means that moisture is coming in through the floor.

To test for moisture infiltration through the foundation walls, tape a piece of aluminum foil to the foundation wall and monitor to see if it develops condensation on the outfacing side.

Basement Space

Yes, there is habitable space to be found in most basements, but the searching can be difficult. Re-allocating storage space requires some thought, and you will encounter many built-in obstacles that define the potential space for a new room. Building codes also set minimum room size and ceiling height restrictions.

Take measurements to evaluate how to manage pipes and ductwork.

Basement Building Codes

If you are considering building a home office, family room/recreation area, or any other habitable space in your basement, review the list of codes with which your project must comply before you invest a lot of time, planning, or money in the job. It is worth a visit to your local building department to discuss your plans with an inspector.

Subjects covered by basement-related codes for habitable rooms include:

- Headroom

- Minimum room size

- Egress (escapability)

- Ventilation

- Lighting

- Electrical service and receptacles

- Electric service panel location

- Proximity to furnaces and major appliances

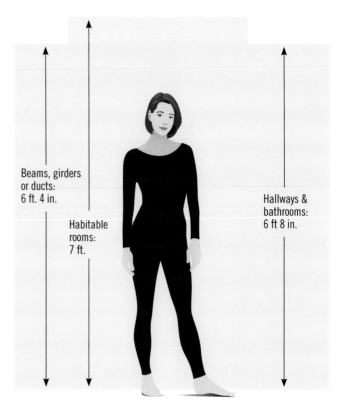

Beams, girders or ducts: 6 ft. 4 in.

Habitable rooms: 7 ft.

Hallways & bathrooms: 6 ft 8 in.

Most habitable rooms require a 7-foot ceiling, with exceptions made for hanging obstructions, such as ductwork. Hallways and bathrooms can have ceilings as low as 6 feet, 8 inches or even less—there is some variance among jurisdictions.

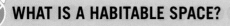

WHAT IS A HABITABLE SPACE?

Precise legal definitions of a habitable space vary, but in general it is simply a space (not necessarily an enclosed room) that is intended for continual human occupancy. Most codes include living, sleeping, dining, and cooking among the activities that constitute occupancy. In most cases, bathrooms, hallways, utility rooms, and closets are not considered habitable and therefore are not subject to the same set of codes.

Basement Headroom

Most basements do not have the minimum 8-foot-high ceilings you will find in the upper stories of your house. This does not exclude them from being habitable; It just might mean taller folks have to learn to duck. In addition to lower ceilings, most basements have ductwork, beams, gas and water/drain pipes, and other obstructions that descend down below ceiling height. According to national building codes, to be suitable for living, the ceiling height should be no lower than 7 feet. Some hanging obstructions are okay as long as they are not closer to the floor than 6 feet, 4 inches. Since ductwork and pipework tend to be located primarily in the floor joist cavities, few hang down lower than this minimum height. Nonliving spaces, such as hallways and bathrooms, can be a short as 6 feet, 8 inches. Codes for your area may specify different minimum distances, so always check with your local building department.

Minimum Basement Room Sizea

Local building departments have minimum standards for how much floorspace a habitable room must have—in general, at least 70 square feet in total floorspace and at least one wall that is a minimum of 7 feet long. In some cases, a kitchen (kitchenette really) may be as small as 50 square feet. Bear in mind that a 70-square-foot room feels very small. Even a 100-square-foot room is considered small.

Egress Window and Window Well Standards

Codes require that any habitable room has at least two avenues for escape in the event of fire or other emergency. The door counts as one. On upper floors, most windows are large enough to escape through if the door were blocked. Most basement windows are too small for this. An allowable egress window must have a minimum opening of $5\frac{7}{10}$ square feet. How this is calculated depends on window type. Single-sash windows, such as casements, count as one opening. But in windows with multiple sashes, such as double-hung or side-by-side sliding windows, you can only count the area of a single sash. And, in addition to the 5.7 square-foot standard, the space you would fit through (a sash) must be at least 20 inches wide and 24 inches high. So, if you are hoping to add habitable space to your basement, it is likely that you may need to replace at least one small basement window with a larger egress window. This is a labor-intensive job that usually requires cutting into your foundation wall and enlarging the window well. If you don't have the experience to do this safely, hire someone who does.

Installing a new window that meets minimum egress rules often means deepening the existing window opening by removing a section of the masonry foundation wall beneath the window opening.

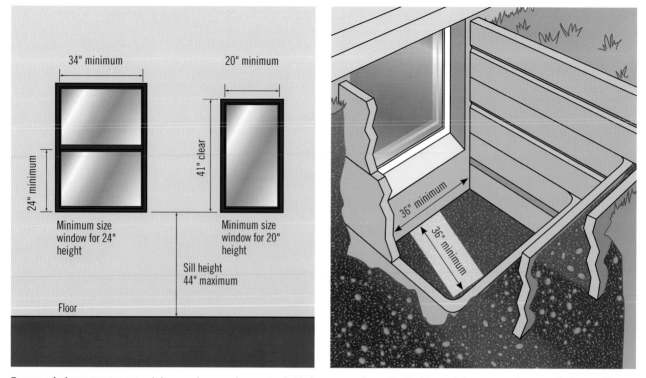

34" minimum   20" minimum

24" minimum

41" clear

Minimum size
window for 24"
height

Minimum size
window for 20"
height

Sill height
44" maximum

Floor

36" minimum

36" minimum

Egress windows must meet minimum size requirements, both for access from the inside and for escape from a window well on the exterior.

Basement Ventilation and Air Quality

Only bathrooms and kitchens have specific ventilation requirements (although clothes dryers and furnaces have their own exhaust ventilation demands). Nevertheless, if your plan is to occupy all or part of your basement, you will need good ventilation for it to be a safe and comfortable space. Most basements are inherently humid, and humidity plus inadequate ventilation encourages mold and mildew growth, which is a health hazard. Plus, a poorly ventilated space has stale or stuffy air, which only becomes more problematic when you introduce breathing inhabitants (i.e., people) and other changes to the environment.

Perhaps the easiest way to improve air quality is to buy and use an air purifier appliance. Fitted with filters, these standalone devices draw in air, filter it, and exhaust it back into the room. They do not improve air humidity. You can also provide mechanical ventilation by installing one or more vent fans that exhaust outside your home. These can work in tandem with added or expanded windows for better natural ventilation, provided windows and doors are left open.

A standalone air purifier with changeable or cleanable filters improves air quality but doesn't solve ventilation issues or address excess humidity.

Basement Lighting and Electrical

Any habitable room must have a light source that is operated by a switch that is reachable from the entry doorway. Storage rooms, hallways, staircases, and utility rooms also must have a switch-operated light source. For practical reasons you'll want to ensure that you have dependable lighting sources in the space, especially since most basements get relatively little natural light.

Electrical service and receptacles. A habitable room must have an electrical outlet every 6 feet along the walls, as well as in utility areas and in every hallway longer than 10 feet. In bathrooms, unfinished spaces, and within 6 feet of a faucet or water source, code requires Ground Fault Circuit Interrupter (GFCI) outlets or circuits. Recent code changes in many areas require GFCI outlets or circuits in all basement locations (as well as garages). Check with your local building inspector.

Electric service panel location. Your main electrical service panel must be accessible and cannot be located in a bathroom or above a stairway. It is okay to build a basement room that encompasses the electrical service panel, but be sure to comply with minimum panel access requirements.

Proximity to furnaces and major appliances. Codes are very specific when it comes to major household plant systems: the heat plant and the cooling plant in particular. When planning an addition or expansion in your basement, keep your project as far from the furnace and the main electrical service panel as you can. If you have the opportunity to integrate the environmental controls of your new basement room into the existing HVAC system, do it. It will ensure reliable airflow and heating/cooling in your new room, but it will also impact the overall heating and cooling in your whole house. It should only be done by or with the input of HVAC professionals.

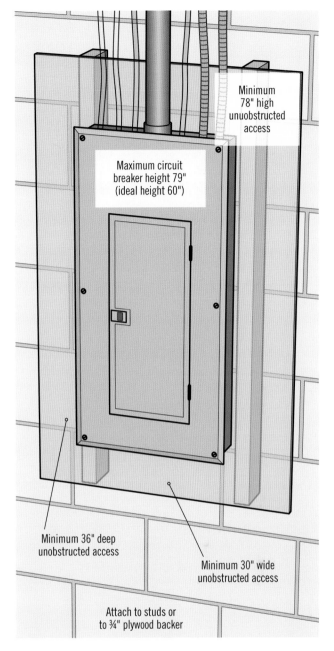

Minimum 78" high unuobstructed access

Maximum circuit breaker height 79" (ideal height 60")

Minimum 36" deep unobstructed access

Minimum 30" wide unobstructed access

Attach to studs or to ¾" plywood backer

If you'll locate your new basement living space near your main electrical service panel, you'll need to make sure not to violate any of these clearance and accessibility codes.

Controlling Basement Moisture

Listen to any call-in home improvement show and it's a pretty good bet that at some point a caller will ask how to address a basement moisture problem. And just as inevitably, the answer the caller receives is essentially "It depends—I'd have to see it." Excess basement moisture is a very common and very serious problem that can have one or more causes.

Most often, water in the basement comes from seepage through the foundation walls or basement floors. Poor drainage around the exterior of the wall could be the culprit: The grade of the soil surrounding the walls should run away from the house at a slope of no less than 1 inch per foot. Regrading is not complicated, but it involves some heavy labor. Adding gutters and downspouts can help: The outlets on the downspouts should be at least 8 feet from the house. You can also add waterproof covers if you are getting excessive water runoff in the window wells.

Cracks and failed joints in foundation walls are another common source of seepage. They are usually easy to identify if you have an active problem. Interior wall paint will peel and flake off. Unpainted masonry foundation walls develop a white, scaly residue called efflorescence. And of course, cracks and physical deterioration, such as spalling, are easy to spot (provided they are not concealed by wallcoverings). All of these cases require repairing the point or points of moisture access. The general idea is to remove as much of the deteriorated masonry as you can and use a cold chisel or other tool to create "keyhole" edges that are wider at the bottom of the damaged area than at the surface of the wall. This helps the concrete repair product stay in place when you apply it. Normally, you will apply a liquid bonding agent (usually latex-based) to the repair surface to further secure the repair product. Use a hydraulic cement-repair product designed for use in damp areas—hydraulic cement actually hardens the more it is exposed to moisture.

Waterproofing coatings, such as the cement/polymer membrane being brushed on here, can help in some situations, but unless you address any bigger, underlying issues, the fix will be temporary at best.

You can trowel hydraulic concrete-repair product into cracks in masonry floors and walls once you have properly prepared the crack.

Window wells generally don't contribute significantly to seepage unless the window's framing or condition is an issue. Clear plastic window well covers can help keep water runoff from accumulating in the well.

Installing a submersible sump pump in a pit that extends beneath the foundation floor is helpful if the ground beneath the foundation has a very high water table that causes seepage up through the floor due to hydrostatic pressure.

In some cases, condensation can be the reason your basement is too damp. This occurs when moist air comes in contact with colder surfaces and forms water droplets on the surface. A dehumidifier (see page 48) is the easiest solution, and adding insulation around the cold surfaces also helps.

A persistent problem that does not noticeably improve when you try the obvious may call for a more radical solution: excavating around the perimeter of the foundation and installing a footing drain; or installing an electric sump pump into the basement floor to pump water from below the floor to a safe, exterior drainage area. Both solutions are fairly complicated, expensive, and probably best left to a pro.

Furred-Out Basement Walls

Furring, where you create a stud wall against or next to the foundation, offers fastening surfaces for drywall or other wallcoverings and creates wall cavities into which you can add insulation and wiring. They are a good way to up the comfort of your basement space.

You have three options when planning your furred-out wall:

• Create a narrow air gap by building an independent stud wall about ½ inch from the foundation wall and fill in between the studs with insulation.

• Attach the wall studs directly to the foundation wall, which is essentially what furring means.

• Apply polystyrene or isocyanurate insulation panels directly to the foundation wall and then build the stud walls so the framing members are flush against the insulation layer.

Insulation and vapor barriers. Other than in the southmost regions of the US, most codes require that you insulate next to your basement wall. Although you can use unfaced fiberglass batts, most remodelers warn against that because these batts trap moisture. A better choice is extruded polystyrene or a closed-cell insulation panel, such as isocyanurate. These products

To make your basement livable, cover any bare masonry foundation walls with something friendlier. Add wall studs to create voids for insulation, cables, and electrical boxes and as a way to attach wallcoverings. It's common to build these "furred" walls with 2 × 3 or even 2 × 2 lumber instead of standard 2 × 4. This isn't a cost-saving tactic as much as it is meant to conserve floorspace. However, if you plan to add plumbing to your new room, a 2 × 4 wall creates a deep enough wall cavity for supply and drain pipes.

One option for a furred-out wall is to install panels of extruded polystyrene against the foundation wall. You can use a non-solvent-based panel adhesive to bond them or simply friction-fit them and rely on the stud wall to pin them in place. Tape the insulation seams with insulation tape, then build the furred-out stud wall up against the insulation. Use treated lumber for the sole plate and attach the plates to the floor with powder-actuated nails. Nail the cap plate to the floor joists above.

stand up better to moisture. Some insulation panel manufacturers offer products that have tongue-and-groove seams that fit together tightly. Once you butt them together, apply insulation tape over the seams of straight-edge panels. As long as they are attached between the foundation and the furred-out stud wall, this will improve the moisture-resistance envelope.

There is quite a bit of debate in the building world whether or not to install a vapor barrier on a furred-out basement wall. The best advice is always to consult with your local building department, because they know best the conditions in your locale. The opponents of vapor barriers between the stud wall and the wallcovering hold that, in the event moisture makes its way through the foundation wall, it will collect in the wall cavity with no means of escape, molding and rotting the wood framing members. It's largely because of this possibility that remodelers prefer to apply foam insulation directly to the wall, where it functions as a vapor retarder but will not trap moisture in the wall cavities.

Another option for a "classic" furred-out wall is to attach the studs directly to the foundation wall with powder-actuated nails. Try to drive the nails away from the mortar joints on block walls. Because the studs are well secured to the wall, you can get away with 2 × 2 lumber to conserve space while still providing fastening points for the wallcoverings.

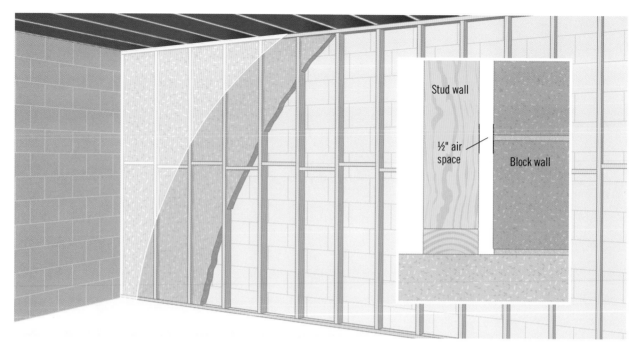

Stud wall

½" air space

Block wall

A third option for making a new basement wall along the foundation walls is to build a standard stud wall about ½ inch out from the foundation wall. This airspace eliminates direct contact between the studs and the foundation wall.

RIM JOISTS

The rim joist rests on top of your foundation wall and provides an attachment point for the ends of the floor joists. It also will create a gap above your new wall that is especially vulnerable to heat/cold transfer, since it generally is above ground. Before you build your furred-out wall, cut pieces of 2-inch-thick rigid, foil-faced isocyanurate insulation and fit them against the rim joist above the wall. It's also not a bad idea to fit pieces of insulation in the voids on top of the foundation wall.

DEALING WITH DUCTWORK

The basement area where you are building your new room probably will have ductwork or other obstructions that drop down below the ceiling level. If it is possible to relocate these so they fit into the joist cavity, do it. If not, you can build a soffit frame around the obstruction and attach wallcovering materials to the frame to conceal the obstruction. You may even be able to add elements, such as canister lights, to the soffit, but be aware you'll need to create an access panel so you can get at the electrical connections if needed.

If you plan to run pipes, gas, or electrical in the furred-out wall, plan ahead and leave a channel in the furring strips to accommodate them.

You must bond the new furred-out wall securely to the basement floor. Use a powder-actuated nailer to drive fasteners through the base plate (2 × 2 or 2 × 4 pressure-treated) and into the concrete.

To maximize living space in your new room, keep the furred walls as thin as possible. In most cases, a 2 × 2 wall framing system will serve fine as a nailing surface for wallcoverings while creating wall cavities through which you can run small elements.

Upgrading Basement Ventilation

Good ventilation is key to creating a comfortable environment anywhere and in a basement situation particularly. Natural ventilation (windows) helps, but you can't count on that day to day. For reliable air movement and ventilation in a basement living situation, you will need the mechanical solution of installing a vent fan or fans. You'll find a number of options, from bathroom-style vent fans to floor-level units that pull air upward, and just about everything in between. Some vent fans, often with twin fans—one intake and one exhaust—are made to fit into basement window openings. Whichever fan type you select, the goal in planning the system is to create airflow that exhausts stale basement air and draws in fresh, clean air to replace it.

Vent Fan Types

For residential use there are several categories of ventilation fan to consider. The simplest solution is to place two or more box fans in the basement to move air and direct it toward an outlet, such as a window. While cheap and easy, this is not a permanent solution and it has other downsides, such as potential tripping hazards and relatively low efficiency rates. Here are a few of the more common, permanent equipment options.

Overhead "bathroom" fan. If you've ever remodeled a bathroom, you have likely installed one or more of these very common devices, probably in the ceiling and operated by a wall switch. The fans are attached to 4-inch-diameter tubing that is typically run between the ceiling joists and hooked up to a vent duct assembly that penetrates the exterior wall and is capped with a vent cover on the outside.

Typical bathroom vent fans, which are required in most bathrooms but can be used in any room, are rated by the amount of air they move. Measured in cubic feet per minute (CFM), air volume ratings start at 50 CFM and can be as high as 300 CFM for in-ceiling, bathroom-style fans. For bathrooms, your vent fan should move one CFM for each square foot of floor space. There is no hard-and-fast rule for non-bathroom spaces, but you can certainly use the 1:1

A ceiling vent fan, or one mounted at the top of a wall or at floor level, provides air movement and exhausts undesirable air impurities.

Window-mount fans fit into an existing window opening in much the same way as a window air conditioner to assist in air movement in or out of the room.

The **CFM rating** of vent fans indicates the amount of air the fan will move and the SONES rating categorizes the amount of noise the unit makes from 1 (quieter) to 7 (louder).

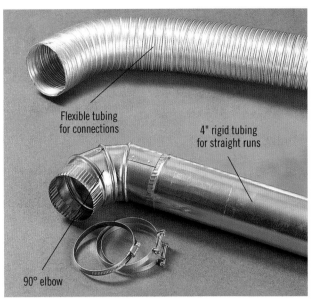

Flexible tubing
for connections

4" rigid tubing
for straight runs

90° elbow

CFM:square-foot ratio for an office or rec room that you are seeking to ventilate. Note that units that have higher CFM ratings tend to be louder. How much noise the fan makes is listed on the fan along with the CFM rating. Expressed in "SONES," it uses a scale of 1 to 7, with lower SONE ratings given to quieter fans.

Through-the-wall ventilation fans. Vent fans that are mounted directly on the exterior wall represent another class of fans with an extremely wide-ranging number of options. In a basement situation, you need to mount these fans to the rim joist and exhaust them to the exterior unless you have a walk-out basement with above-grade walls. This fan type is very efficient and requires less ductwork installation. You can also get programmable models that can turn on and off based on the room's air temperature and humidity levels. This cuts down on noise an unnecessary energy use.

Most codes allow flexible foil/metallic (aluminum) tubing vent ducts, which are good for connecting directly to the fan unit and navigating turns. Enclosed runs mostly require rigid metal (aluminum or galvanized steel) tubing, which is harder to work with and requires elbow connectors. Flexible plastic or vinyl tubing, while still sold in some areas, is not generally allowed by most codes and is particularly ill-suited for venting dryers.

Window-mount fans. A window fan is designed to fit into a window opening much as a window air conditioner unit does. Mostly installed temporarily in upper-level windows in non-air-conditioned rooms, the profile of most models allows installation in standard basement windows. Some are reversible so you can draw in fresh air or expel damp, musty air.

Basement vent fans usually exhaust through a louvered vent pipe assembly with a tail piece that extends through the rim joist and into the joist channels in the basement, where it connects to the ductwork from the fan unit.

Before

After

Many basement windows no longer open or never did. If your basement windows are rotted, in poor repair, or simply don't open, consider replacing them with new, operable windows to add some natural ventilation to your basement.

Replacing small basement windows with larger egress windows (and accompanying window wells) opens up many new options for habitability, but replacing failed or under-performing windows with new ones that can let some breeze in has great benefits too.

Replacing Basement Windows

In addition to the moisture and wind that attack any window, basement windows are vulnerable to ground contact and such things as croquet balls and kickballs that don't normally threaten higher windows. Under such stress, they stop working right.

If you are planning to occupy your basement in a meaningful way, take a look at the existing windows: Replacing them with fresh windows that can actually provide ventilation is pretty easy.

Remove the old window and frame and install a new rough frame, including header, footer, and side jambs. Apply plenty of caulk to the frame members before nailing them in place with a powder-actuated tool.

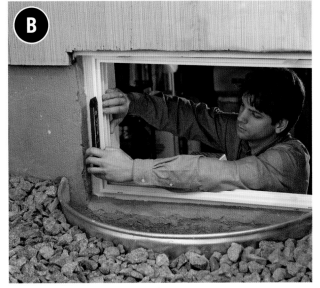

Set the new window frame into the opening. Get it level and square, which is easier to do if you remove the glass sash.

Drive screws through the new window frame to install it in the frame opening.

Seal the gaps around the window with expandable spray foam and then fill gaps around the window with caulk. Attach moldings around the exterior to cover the gaps around the window.

Basement Floors

Most common floorcoverings should not be laid directly onto a concrete floor, especially in a basement, with its inevitable moisture issues. A buffer layer of subfloor helps tremendously and it is easy to create one. The subfloor layer needs to offer breathability and a means for moisture to escape. Because basement rooms generally face ceiling-height limitations, you may not have the option to lay down a subfloor that raises the floor enough to impinge on the room height restrictions.

Before you get too far into your flooring deliberations, inspect the basement floor thoroughly looking for defects in the concrete and signs of moisture penetration. You must address these before you install new floorcoverings (see page 54).

As a general rule, look for floorcoverings that perform well in damp situations, such as resilient vinyl sheets or tiles or planks. These products not only resist damage from moisture; they also provide a less hospitable environment for mold and mildew growth. But they are not your only option. Engineered wood products, such as wood laminate strip flooring or tiles, can be used with an appropriate underlayment. Choosing basement-friendly products and installation techniques allows you to add the warmth of carpeting to your basement environments. But whichever floorcovering you choose, how well it performs depends on what is underneath it.

Four of the many options for creating a warm and welcoming basement floor are, clockwise from top left: Interlocking raised subfloor panels with closed-cell foam underlayment and wood laminate strip flooring; Subfloor panels with cementboard underlayment and ceramic tile (if your basement floor is in good shape you may be able to set the tiles into a mortar bed applied directly to the floor); Subfloor panels with ¼-inch plywood underlayment and resilient sheet flooring or tiles; Treated 2 × 4 sleepers laid flat over a plastic vapor barrier and covered with ¾-inch plywood subfloor and attached-back carpeting that can be rolled up and removed if it gets wet.

Basement Floorcovering Options

Floating laminate or vinyl plank floors are engineered strips or planks with tongue-and-groove edges that snap together. Install this over a thin underlayment laid onto a sturdy subfloor, not concrete. Solid vinyl strips and planks are installed much the same way and hold up better in moist conditions.

Resilient vinyl tiles have been popular basement floor options for many years. Some are solid "homogenous" tiles, usually around 12 × 12 inches, set into mastic. Others are self-adhesive, with a paper backing you remove prior to sticking them to a smooth underlayment. Once limited, patterns and styles now available are more on-trend with design styles.

Ceramic or porcelain tile has been a favorite for basement floors for a long time, largely because of their resistance to moisture and related mold/mildew issues. If your concrete floor is level and in good repair, you can install them in thin-set mortar applied directly to the floor. If not, install a subbase of plywood subfloor or subfloor panels topped with cementboard or tileboard (shown above). Style, size, and shape options have expanded greatly in this product category too.

Carpet and carpet square face some limitations in a moist setting such as a basement floor, but if you are drawn to the underfoot warmth and softness they provide, you can use them in a basement room—as long as you do some careful preparation. You'll need a subfloor with either an allowance for air movement or a contiguous vapor barrier below. You'll get better results if you add an underlayment (usually ¼-inch plywood) between the subfloor and the carpet treatment.

Radiant floors provide heat that emanates up through the flooring. Wire heating elements imbedded in a concrete underlayment heat some and others rely on pneumatic tubing filled with heated liquid. While great for a bathroom, they may be cost prohibitive for a large basement room. Consider them if you are looking for a way to heat a cold room without having an impact on the air environment. This is not normally a DIY project.

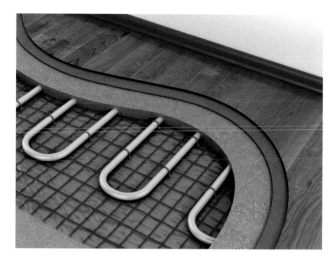

Resurfacing a Basement Floor

Concrete is one of the most durable building materials, but it can degrade in basement conditions. For the best results when installing a new floor in your basement environment, you may need to do some prep work. After repairing any cracks or holes (see page 67), pour on a concrete resurfacer to make the surface accommodating to new flooring. Floor resurfacer is a cement-based product you can buy at most building centers. Because it is still a liquid when you apply it, this material evens out the floor by flowing to the lower areas. When it hardens you will be left with a smooth, level base on which you can install your floor.

Before

After

Applying floor resurfacer to a concrete floor creates a smooth, level surface to use as a sturdy base for supporting floorcoverings or to serve as the surface itself with the right sealer, acid, paint, or other finishing product.

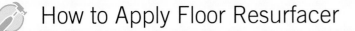# How to Apply Floor Resurfacer

TOOLS AND MATERIALS
Pressure washer or stiff-bristle brush
Concrete cleaning solution
Concrete resurfacer
5-gallon bucket
Long-handled squeegee

1. Make your floor as clean and debris-free as possible. This is a good application for a pressure washer, but if you don't have access to one, use a stiff-bristle brush and concrete cleaning solution to remove any grime or grease. There's no need to let the floor dry.

2. Fill any holes or cracks with a stiff mixture of the resurfacer product (Photo A). Follow product directions on how much water to use. Rinse the floor with clean water.

3. In a clean 5-gallon bucket, mix the floor resurfacer with water to a syrupy, pourable consistency. Follow product directions on how much water to use.

4. Spray on more water as necessary to dampen the floor.

5. Working in sections no larger than 100 square feet, pour out resurfacer mixture near the center of the work area (Photo B).

6. Spread the mixture over the floor with a long-handled squeegee to help it find its level, which it will do before it hardens (Photo C). Don't apply in layers thicker than ½ inch; try to avoid ridges or valleys. If necessary, apply a second coat after the first coat has set up for a few hours. **Let it cure at least a day before walking on it**.

Trowel a stiff mixture of the concrete resurfacer into any holes, divots, or low areas before you pour resurfacer at its regular consistency.

Work in 100-sq.-ft. sections when pouring the resurfacer mix.

Spread the mixture across the floor evenly using a long-handled squeegee. Don't apply layers more than ½-inch thick. Let it cure for at least a day before walking on it.

How to Install Raised Subfloor Panels

You have a number of options when creating a subfloor in your basement, but perhaps the easiest is to lay interlocking raised subfloor panels. Typically 24 × 24 inches, the panels have a plastic grid on the underside to allow airflow and a plywood or oriented-strand board surface.

If you have ever installed floor tile, the process for installing raised subfloor panels will seem familiar. It involves creating a layout design that maximizes the number of tongue-and-groove joints while keeping cuts to a minimum.

TOOLS AND MATERIALS
Measuring tape
Subfloor panels
¼-inch-thick spacers
Level
Shims
Utility knife
Straightedge
Mallet
Tapping block
Pull bar

1. Measure your floor space and use your panel size to calculate the number of tiles and the best placement for them.

2. Place ¼-inch-thick spacers next to the walls and set the first panel into place with the tongue side fitting flat against the spacers. Slide in the next panel, creating the tongue-and-groove joint (Photo A).

3. Continue installing panels to fill out the first row. Check for level as you go and shim beneath the panels if necessary so they form a flat surface.

4. Start a perpendicular row of panels along an adjoining wall. Cut the panels in half to stagger the row seams. Use a mallet and tapping block to secure the panels (Photo B).

5. Cut the last row of panels to fit, preserving the tongue-and-groove profiles where possible. Use a pull bar to snug the last panels tightly against the adjoining row (See Photo C).

The tongue-and-groove edges of raised subfloor panels click together into a uniform subfloor surface that is a suitable underlayment for just about any basement floorcovering.

Start laying in the panels with the tongue sides of the first panel against the ¼-inch spacers. Add the next panel.

Cut panels in half for a row that's perpendicular to the first. Use a mallet and tapping block to rap the panels together.

Install the final row of panels and draw the joints tightly together with a pullbar.

Basement Ceilings

Your new basement room will likely need a ceiling. This creates some logistical issues that can cause any remodeler to think hard about the best approach.

A drop-down ceiling typically lowers the ceiling height by about 3 inches, but they're a practical solution if you can afford the vertical space. Most basement renovations use the joists that support the first floor to house wiring, plumbing, HVAC ductwork, and gas pipes. Suspended panels make it easy to access any of these mechanical systems. Provided you are working with products designed for it, it's also fairly easy to cut in for light fixtures and ceiling-mounted vent fans in a suspended ceiling.

If vertical space is at a premium, you can attach drywall or paneling directly to the joists to keep the downward intrusion on room spaces to as little as ¼ to ⅝ inches. With this solution, codes will very likely require you to install multiple access panels in the ceiling to let you get at any shutoffs (water or gas supply) or junction boxes in the joist cavities above.

Ceiling panels installed in a framework of track suspended from or attached to the ceiling joists allow you to route wiring and plumbing in the joist cavities and still retain easy access to them.

Basement Ceiling Options

Traditional acoustic tile has tongue-and-groove edges and is formed from mineral/fiber material. You can install it with a track system or staple it to wood battens attached to the ceiling joists. It is relatively inexpensive, but the patterns and colors are limited and it is not moisture or mold resistant if your basement has humidity issues.

Drywall, ½- or ⅝-inch thick, creates a permanent ceiling surface that does not significantly detract from room height. You can install it working alone if you rent a drywall lifter or create one or more "deadmen," which are 2 × 4 T-shaped aides slightly longer than the room height that you can assemble and used to prop up the sheet goods (inset).

WRAP PIPES AND DUCTWORK

If you will be capturing any pipes or ductwork in the joist cavities above the ceiling, insulate them before installing the ceiling materials. Wrap water supply pipes with foam pipe insulation (available at most building centers) to help prevent them from forming condensation that can drip onto the ceiling panels.

Suspended ceilings hang in a framework of metal channels and create space above to run home mechanicals. They are sold in either 24 × 24-inch or 24 × 48-inch panels in a slightly wider variety of styles than acoustic tile. You can also add light troffer inserts that are sized to fit neatly into the framework.

Installing Suspended Ceilings

Installing a suspended ceiling in a basement room is relatively easy but does require some patience and careful measuring. The trick is to square up the spaces in the framework where the drop-in panels fit and size them correctly. Once you have the framework installed and in good shape, the installation of the panels is a snap. If you are incorporating panel lights, ceiling fans, canister lights, or other ceiling elements, install them before you install the panels.

Suspended ceiling hung from wire-supported metal tracks easily integrates with canister lights, ceiling fans, and other ceiling elements and allows access to the joist cavities.

SUSPENDED CEILINGS AND BASEMENT WINDOWS

When installing a drop-down ceiling in a basement, one common challenge is that the tops of typical basement hopper windows may well be higher than the finished elevation of the drop-down ceiling. Rather than simply having your ceiling terminate partway up the window, the better solution is to build a valance around the top of the window on the interior side. This is done by building a 3-sided frame around the window top with 1× stock so the bottoms of the frame are at the same height as the panel framework. Then, you can attach the wall angle that supports the panels directly to the underside of the frame and support the panels on the wall angle. You'll probably want to close off the top of the frame by attaching drywall or a cutoff piece of the ceiling panel material at the top of the frame.

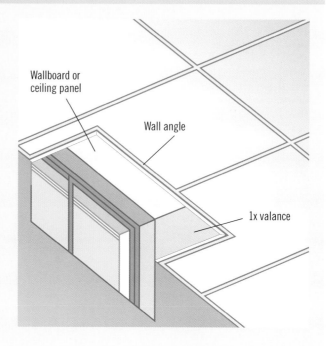

Wallboard or ceiling panel

Wall angle

1x valance

How to Install a Suspended Basement Ceiling

Select the panel system you want to install. You will need the panels as well as the wall angle, which are L-shaped metal tracks that attach to the walls and support the main beams and cross tees, which in turn support the drop-in ceiling panels. These materials mostly are sold in cartons or kits. All include specific estimation and installation instructions that will help you calculate how many of each you need based on your planned layout. You'll also need wire (12 gauge is adequate for most ceilings) and hooks that screw into the ceiling joists to hold the wires that then fit into predrilled holes in the beams. As for tools, you'll need:

TOOLS AND MATERIALS

Tape measure

Chalkline

Laser level

Drill/driver

Aviator snips

Combination square

Lock clamps (specialty clamp for suspended ceiling frames)

Mason's line

Utility knife

Drywall framing square

Spring clamps

Pop riveter

A suspended ceiling makes sense in many basements—it hides plumbing and wiring and lends a more finished and intentional feeling to the space below.

Make a plan. Take measurements, read the manufacturer's layout instructions provided with your suspended ceiling system, and draw out a plan. If you need to cut ceiling panels (which is very likely), arrange your cuts so the cut panels only fall at the borders and the rows of cut panels are even on each side of the room. Note that the main beams should be installed perpendicular to the ceiling joists and spaced the correct distance apart to support uncut panels. If you will be installing a light or vent fan in the suspended ceiling, do the wiring work before you begin installing the ceiling. Do not hook the wring up to live current yet.

Install wall angle. The L-shaped wall angle anchors the drop-down ceiling and establishes its height and level. The bottoms of the wall angle pieces should be at least 3 inches below the ceiling joists. If your ceiling dips or is not level, measure down from the lowest point and mark the height. Use a laser level as a guide to make height marks all around the walls of the room. Attach the metal wall angle at wall stud locations with 1½-inch drywall screws. These self-tapping screws generally do not require pilot holes to get through the light-gauge metal of the wall angle.

Install the main beams. The main beams support the field area of the ceiling. They are suspended from the ceiling joists and should be spaced to match the panel width according to your plan. As a guide, string taut mason's lines between wall angles at the opposite sides of the room. A specialty tool called a lock clamp is made just for this job. You can find them with ceiling tools and supplies at your local building center. Clamp one to a wall angle at a main beam location and tie a mason's line to the metal loop on the lock clamp (Photo A). This allows the line to align perfectly with the edge of the wall angle. Repeat at the opposite wall and measure to make sure the clamps are spaced correctly and the line is square to the wall angles.

The instructions for your ceiling system usually specify the minimum spacing for the wires that are used to support the main beams. In most cases you will not have to install one at each joist.

1. Following the spacing recommendations, insert a screw eye into each ceiling joist directly above the mason's line.

2. Insert a short length of wire (12-gauge is frequently specified) into the screw eye and twist it in securely so a few inches extend past the mason's line.

3. Use a piece of main beam as a guide to bend up the untied end of the wire so that, when it is inserted into a hanger hole in the beam, the bottom of the beam will be level with the mason's line.

The main beams are predrilled with wire hanger holes at regular intervals in the spine, as well as slots into which the ends of the cross tees will fit. Before hanging the beam, check the slot locations against the planned cross tee locations. In most cases, you'll have to trim the end of the beam so that when the end is flush against the wall angle the slots will line up exactly with the cross tees that will snap into them.

1. Use aviator snips to trim the beams.

2. Insert the bent hanger wires into the closest wire hole to the screw eye and twist the wires to secure it. The bottom of the beam should align with the mason's line.

3. Hang the beams in the first row and then move the mason's line and clamps to the next beam location and repeat the process until all beams are hung (Photo B).

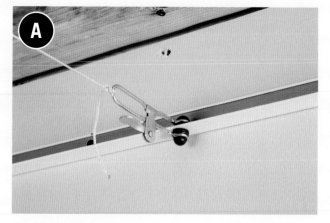

Use a lock clamp, which is a specialty clamp for installing suspended ceiling grids, and a mason's line to set the locations for the main beams.

Hang the main beams with bent wire suspended by screw eyes in the ceiling joists. Trim the beams so the slots for the cross tees fall at the planned cross tee locations. (You may need to remove the mason's line temporarily for access).

SPECIALTY SCREW EYES

Instead of a standard screw eye, look for specialty adjustable wire hangers that are sold with the installation kits and can be purchased along with your ceiling system components. These have screw threads at the top and a tab with a wire guide hole at the bottom. They provide sturdy support and are easy to adjust up or down by turning once you attach the wires. Your store might also sell driver bits that have a slotted opening designed to fit over and spin the hanger with a drill/driver or cordless impact driver.

C

Snap the tabs at the ends of the cross tees into the appropriate slots in the beams to fill out the grid.

D

Use pop rivets to secure the cut cross tees to the wall angle ledge.

Install the cross tees. The cross tees are sized in length to match the width of the ceiling panels—usually 24 inches. They have tabs that are shaped to snap into the slots in the main beams. Begin snapping the cross tees in place with each end inserted into a main beam slot (Photo C). You should not have to cut them. The wall angles do not have slots for the cross tees. Cut cross tees to fit in the narrower rows at the walls. Be sure to leave one of the cross tee ends uncut so you can fit the tab into the main beam slot. The cut end should rest on the ledge of the wall angle. Test to make sure it is square to the wall angle and attach it by drilling a guide hole through both pieces and installing a pop rivet (Photo D). You should be able to find pop rivets with heads the same color as the wall angle—almost always white.

Install the ceiling panels. Most of the ceiling panels will not require cutting if you have laid out the grid framework carefully. Simply slip the end of each panel up through an opening in the grid at an angle (this is why the ceiling needs to be at least 3 inches below the joists) (Photo E). Handle the panels with care as they are quite fragile around the edges. When you have filled in all of the field tiles, cut tiles to fit in the openings along the borders. To cut tiles, place them face-up on a flat surface and score a cutting line with a utility knife and straightedge (a drywall framing square is perfect for this job). Make the score fairly deep and then snap the tile along the scored line. Because most tiles have a reveal along all edges to allow the tiles to be even with the exposed grid once they are installed, you'll need to create a same-side recessed ledge along all cut edges. Do this by making a straight, ½-inch deep cut located ½ inch in from each cut edge. From the side, carefully remove the waste material with your utility knife to create a smooth, straight edge to rest on the grid members (Photo F). Install the cut border tiles (Photo G).

If you are installing lights or fans in the ceiling, make the connections and install them now (Photo H).

Install a ceiling panel into the grid by lifting the panel up into the opening and then lowering it onto the support ledges.

After cutting border tiles to size, cut a ½ × ½-inch shoulder into each cut edge to recreate the reveal that you trimmed off when cutting.

Install the cut border panels last to fill out the ceiling panels. This requires some care and patience to avoid breaking panel edges or dislocating the grid parts.

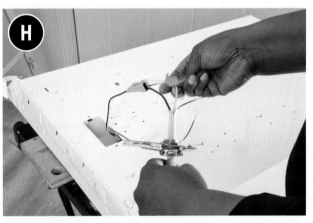

Install ceiling elements, such as lights and fans. The light here is designed to fit into a 2 x 2 suspended ceiling grid (also see page 71 bottom).

Installing Direct-Mounted Basement Ceiling Panels

Direct-mounted ceiling tiles can provide a visual upgrade to a basement room and, in the case of acoustic tile, noise dampening. They are relatively easy to install compared to other ceiling panel systems. Traditional acoustic tiles are made of fiberboard, often with a textured or dimpled surface. More recent products include thin tiles formed from solid PVC that are slightly lower in profile and much lighter. The PVC tiles come in a wider variety of patterns and sizes and generally are suspended in PVC tracks. Runner strips snapped over the framework grid conceal fasteners and make a more finished appearance.

As with suspended ceilings (page 74), you'll want to carefully read the manufacturer's instructions for the tile system you select before you get started. Installation methods vary. Systems that involve a support grid are in many ways more forgiving than panels that you bond or attach directly without a framework, since you can compensate for minor irregularities in your ceiling or ceiling joists when you install the grid.

You can attach direct-mounted ceiling panels with staples or nails to 1 × 2 furring strips fastened to the ceiling joists or mount them in low-profile tracks screwed or stapled to the joists, as with thin PVC tiles. Alternatively, you can bond them with adhesive to an old drywall or plaster ceiling to give it some relief and an updated look.

MAKING A LAYOUT PLAN

It is important to draw out a detailed installation plan before you begin installing your ceiling. Most manufacturer's instructions provide helpful tips for creating a layout that minimizes cutting and results in border rows that are even in width and not too narrow. This is especially important if you are working with tiles that have a distinct pattern or "raised panel" appearance with relief lines.

To determine the border row width, measure the length and width of the ceiling.

- If your measurements are in whole feet and you are using 12 × 12 tile, you can probably install the ceiling without cutting.

- If you are using 24 × 24-inch tile, an even number of whole feet should allow for no cutting (you may want to factor this in when choosing your tile).

- If the measurement is not in whole feet, add 12 to the number of leftover inches (e.g., if the measurement is

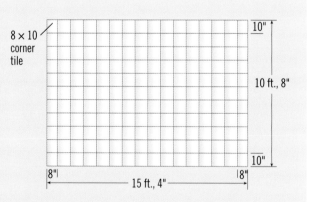

15 feet, 4 inches, add 12 to the 4). Divide the sum of inches and 12 by two to yield an even width of both border rows. In this example, 4 + 12 ÷ 2 = 8, so the rows at each end of the run will need to be 8 inches wide.

How to Install Direct-Mounted Ceiling Panels

TOOLS AND MATERIALS
Ceiling panels
U-shaped wall brackets
Drywall screws
Chalkline
Square
Hanger tracks
Cross tees
Saw
Aviator snips or sharp scissors
Runner strips

1. Make your layout plan (see previous page) and read the manufacturer's installation directions.

2. Attach the U-shaped wall brackets to the wall studs or ceiling joists at the wall/ceiling joint with drywall screws. Be careful not to drive them in too far and kink the plastic brackets (Photo A).

3. Refer to your plan and snap chalklines on the ceiling or ceiling joists to represent the locations for the ceiling tracks. Check to make sure your chalklines are square.

4. Attach the hanger tracks perpendicular to the joists at 12- or 24-inch intervals, depending on panel size (Photo B).

5. Use one of the short cross tees as a spacer to position the next row of hanger tracks. The ends of the cross tees fit into notches on the hanger tracks. Begin installing the second hanger tracks, using another cross tee at the next notch position and driving drywall screws as you go. Continue until you install all of the cross tees and hangers.

6. Cut the cross tees for the border rows to fit and rest the free ends in the U-shaped wall channels.

7. Fit the panels over the support ledges on the hangers and cross tees and begin filling out the field tiles (Photo C).

8. Cut the border tiles to size with aviator snips or sharp scissors and fit them into the grid spaces in the border row.

9. Cap off the hanger tracks with runner strips that fit into the notches on the tracks (Photo D). These will conceal the tracks and help tie the ceiling system together structurally as well as visually.

Use drywall screws to attach the U-shaped wall channels at the junction between the top of the wall and the ceiling.

Attach the first row of hanger tracks perpendicular to the ceiling joists, with the ends inserted into the wall channels.

Begin installing the full-size field panels by fitting them into the grid openings so they rest on the hanger track ledges.

Finish the installation by snapping the runner strips into the slots in the hanger strips.

Closet Offices

The idea of converting a closet into a hardworking space for office labors and homework may sound like a path to creating a cheerless workspace. But recently it has become a popular strategy for expanding the utility of your home. In fact, some have even taken to calling these improvised offices "cloffices." It is possible to convert 20+ square feet of closet space into a viable and even inviting home office, whatever you call it. And perhaps best of all, once you are done working for the day, you can simply close the closet doors and step back into home life without another thought.

Most of the closets in homes today are "reach-in" closets that are 24- to 28-inches deep—just enough room from front to back to allow you to hang clothes and jackets on a central closet rod. But it is also deep enough to contain a desk or custom worksurface. Closet widths vary of course, but in general the space between the door opening and the side walls of the closet is 12 inches or less so you can access the whole closet without stepping into it. There is no minimum size a closet must offer to make it a suitable office space, but of course the larger it is, the more functionality and comfort you can build into the project.

If you are fortunate, you may have a walk-in closet at your disposal. A typical walk-in closet boasts a generous 7 × 10-foot space—plenty of room for a desk and some storage and even a comfortable chair. Walk-ins that are 100 square feet or bigger exist in some higher-end homes, and if you are willing to sacrifice the storage, there is a lot you can do with that space.

One question you will encounter is whether or not to leave the closet door in place. On the plus side, an office door is almost always a good thing. You likely won't be able to have it closed while you work, but its presence does allow you to close off the office from your normal household life. On the other hand, a door does pose some restrictions. A bifold closet door impedes on the side-to-side space available when you are occupying the doorway with your office chair. Without modifications, such as being able to fold it out of the way, any door will restrict you from extending your worksurface past the door opening.

If you have a very small closet, it can make sense to relegate the closet area to storage and perhaps peripherals such as printers and scanners. This would allow you to set up a desk or workstation anywhere in the general proximity.

Finishing the closet walls with wallpaper or paneling, or just a fresh coat of paint, is a good starting point.

This closet office did not require a great deal of makeover, just a shallow ledge shelf and a desk and chair.

A closet office can include a desk and chair, or if you have shallower closets, it may be as simple as rearranging the space for shelving and storing office supplies and documents.

You can set up a functional office inside of a closet or even next to one to take advantage of unused space and the outer closet wall.

Closet Office Conversion

The specific steps you will need to take to convert any closet to office space depends, of course, on what you have to work with. But the overall steps share some commonality regardless of whether you are dealing with a small bedroom closet or a walk-in closet. Typical closets are around 30 inches deep and range from 3 to 8 feet wide. In most cases, it makes sense to construct a built-in desktop that is supported by the closet walls and runs the full width and depth. Standard desktop height is 32 inches. You can add shelving to the walls above the desktop and, if you have the space, include room for file cabinets underneath. If you are really ambitious, make your own built-in cabinets, but leave adequate space for a desk chair and your legs.

Start by cleaning out everything. If your closet has overhead lighting, consider replacing the bare-bulb fixture with something more useful, such as a small track-lighting fixture. Also consider adding an electrical outlet.

Once the closet is empty and clean, direct your attention to the walls and ceiling. At the very least,

paint the walls so they are a different color from the walls in the surrounding room. It's a naturally dark space, so a lighter color generally makes more sense. Or, you can even get a little fancy and install wallcoverings or paneling to set the space apart (Photo A).

Install overhead shelving before you install a worksurface. There are many ways to go about this, from simple shelf brackets to elaborate cleats (Photo B). The main thing is to avoid making the shelves too deep—12 to 16 inches is plenty for most storage purposes and won't restrict you from accessing the upper shelves.

In most cases it is best to support your worksurface with wall-mounted cleats (Photo C), leaving as much under-desk space as possible. Size a double layer of plywood or medium-density fiberboard (MDF) custom desktop to fit the space. You can add front-edge trim made from 1 × 2 lumber to the desktop and paint it or even apply a layer of plastic laminate to the top for a smooth, washable, and more attractive surface.

 WHAT ABOUT POWER?

Most closets do not contain a power outlet, although some do have hard-wired overhead lighting. If you are making a closet into an office, you can probably get by with an extension cord. For a more elegant and long-lasting solution, add an electrical receptacle to the back wall of the closet, preferably above desk height. This is a good job for an electrician, but if you have some good DIY skills, you can find information on how to add on to an existing circuit in any good home wiring book. You can even avoid the need to run cable through your walls by using surface-mounted raceway to add a receptacle (page 36).

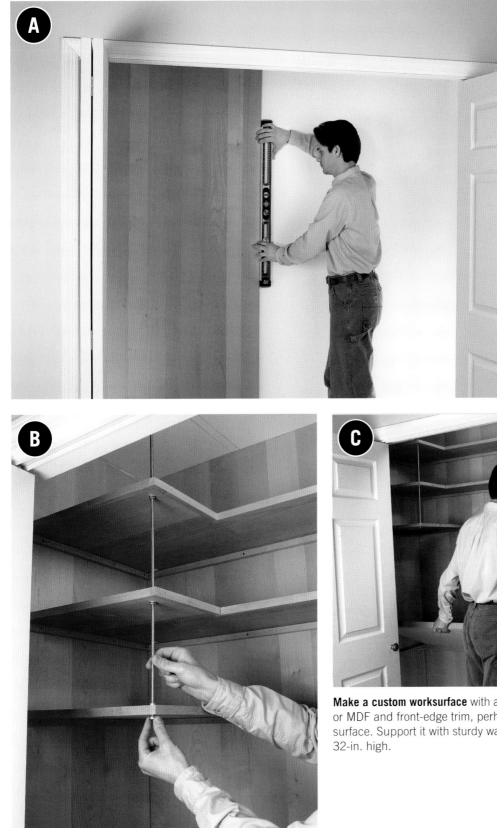

Modify the closet walls to set them apart from the rest of the room by painting or adding attractive paneling.

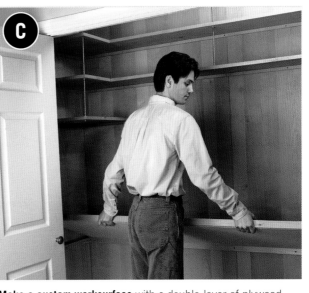

Make a custom worksurface with a double-layer of plywood or MDF and front-edge trim, perhaps with a laminate surface. Support it with sturdy wall cleats so it is about 32-in. high.

Attach cleats to the walls and threaded rod to the ceiling to support shelving. Drill guide holes in the shelves and thread nuts onto the rod.

Creating Living Space in a Garage

Garages vary wildly in the US, from rundown, single-stall standalones to immaculate three-stall attached garages that dominate the façade of your house. But whatever your situation, if you are strapped for living space, your garage can offer a solution. Cars and lawnmowers have different needs than people, however, and most garages are not designed or built to support prolonged human occupation. You can fix this.

Garages perform a handful of utilitarian functions, primarily as homes for our motor vehicles. Depending on other available space, the garage is also where we keep our lawnmowers, snowblowers, chains saws, and other outdoor power equipment. Garages house bicycles, sporting goods, tools, car care products, recyclables and garbage containers, and just about anything that doesn't seem like something we want to keep in the house proper. Useful yes, but their function also sets the garage apart from the home. Take another look and consider your priorities. With relatively little expense and effort, you can clean, insulate, wire, and otherwise improve your garage space to make it comfortable for your people, too. Here are just a few of the possibilities when you upgrade your garage:

- Exercise room/home gym
- Entertainment area
- Workshop/crafting area
- Home office
- Photo/video studio
- Storage space
- Auxiliary food prep area or center for home brewing, winemaking, fermentation
- Pet-grooming spa

With some environmental improvements, you can create entertainment, exercise, or office/study space in a little-used garage or an extra stall in a larger garage.

The garage can become the ultimate multipurpose room, with some planning. Kids going stir-crazy indoors? Back out the car and roll in the fold-up ping-pong table stored in the corner to create a fun space to unwind in the fresh air.

Garage Renovation Potential

The owner of this renovated garage in Florida reclaimed it to create a tidy workshop area and an impressive personal area that can double as a remote workspace.

An auxiliary food prep area in the garage takes pressure off your kitchen and keeps certain activities out of the house, including brewing and winemaking, fish-cleaning, grill prep, canning, and fermenting. You can also use it for entertaining if you choose to add some tables and seating. A sink and faucet provide a useful dimension if you can maintain above-freezing temperatures year-round.

A home gym is a good fit for a garage, especially given the large footprint many exercise machines require. With a nice, clean space and good ventilation, you can enjoy a workout or provide some recess from studies for the kids. Good planning can allow for moving the exercise equipment aside when not in use.

Garage Renovation Considerations

How important is your car, or are your cars, to you? It's okay to answer "very," as next to our houses our vehicles are the biggest investments most of us make. This is the most obvious issue when considering a garage renovation. The longer we live in a house, the more likely our clutter is to take over the garage. Your remodel plan may permanently evict vehicles in favor of human occupancy or split the available space between the car and your remodel project. It may even be possible to remodel in such a way that your car has a home when you aren't using the garage for other purposes. Whatever you choose, you end up with a hardworking home space.

Another consideration while contemplating a garage project is resale value. Garage parking is ranked as a highly desirable feature for prospective homebuyers, so making permanent changes that diminish or remove the ability to park vehicles can work against you when you put your house on the market. It can be wise to choose reversible improvements or ones that still allow the use of the garage for its intended purpose.

Finally, evaluate the general condition of your garage space. Are the walls and floors sound and free of mold? Is the roof in good repair? It makes no sense to embark on an ambitious garage renovation project if you have underlying moisture, rot, or general disrepair issues. You need to deal with these before you begin any remodeling project.

If clutter has taken over your garage, tricks and systems can help you get it under control.

OPTIONS FOR IMPROVING YOUR GARAGE SPACE

If you are thinking of renovating your garage to create new, enclosed living space, then you have a number of options. Here are a few:

- Simple cleaning and decluttering

- Adding wall and ceiling coverings

- Updating storage capabilities to increase efficiency and create more open space

- Cleaning and improving the garage floor by pressure washing, acid washing (etching), making concrete repairs, and/or painting with garage floor paint or epoxy

- Insulating walls and adding wallcoverings

- Upgrading electrical service and lighting

- Improving ventilation

- Weatherizing doors and windows

- Enlarging or adding windows

- Replacing a garage door with one with clear panels

- Adding heating and cooling functionality

This well-used office space highlights a potential benefit of the locale: In a garage, you can stack and pack however you choose.

The Garage Door

Unless you plan to wall off the opening (a fairly radical approach), your garage door is an important part of your interior garage space. Depending on your needs, you can open the door all the way to bring in fresh air and light or close it to protect the interior environment. Consider replacing a door that is in poor repair.

Natural light often is lacking in a garage. If you will be spending a lot of time in the space, consider investing in a garage door that features clear panels. You'll pay a premium, and you should consider the potential security risk of offering a view to the outside world, but you'll also be thankful for the extra light. It's more common to find doors with clear pieces along the top panel of the sectional door, which still let in more natural light than a windowless door.

Whether you install a new door or revamp an existing one, make sure the weatherstripping on the bottom of the lowest door panel is in good condition and forms a good seal with the garage floor apron. This prevents water from running into the garage, blocks cold drafts, and keeps out insects.

Changing to a garage door with windows, even if they are only in the top section, increases the natural light of the space.

How to Replace Garage Door Weatherstripping

If your existing garage weatherstripping is not making a good seal with the concrete apron, replace it. Most building centers carry a variety of products sized for single or double doors and reflecting multiple installation methods. Some are designed with beveled ridges on top that slide into slots in the door panel bottom (see photo at right). Others are designed to be nailed in place. For nail-on weatherstripping, simply remove the old weather stripping with a prybar (Photo A) and then replace it by nailing fresh rubber weatherstripping to the underside of the panel (Photo B).

However you use your garage, its door needs good weatherstripping. Some use a custom slot in the bottom door panel, while others attach with mechanical fasteners.

Remove worn weatherstripping with a prybar. Pull any nails that were used to fasten it.

Purchase new weatherstripping with the same profile as the old and at the correct length for the width of your garage door. Some come with attachment kits others you nail to the door bottom with roofing nails. Follow the directions on the type you purchase.

Improving Garage Lighting

Most garage lighting is not designed or expected to perform like lighting in the living areas of your house. A single hanging fluorescent troffer or a simple overhead bulb often is the only illumination you'll find. It is adequate for helping you find and get into your car safely, but not much more. If you have ever tried to work on the motor of your car or lawnmower using only the extant garage lighting, you'll agree.

Light sources in any room fall into three categories:

- *Primary lighting* is meant to illuminate the entire room as evenly as possible. It is almost always accomplished with ceiling-mounted fixtures and can come from a single or multiple sources. One or more wall switches near the door or doors control this light source. In some cases, a motion detector device may be set up to trigger it.

- *Task lighting*, also called secondary lighting, is directed at specific areas to illuminate specific activities. If ceiling-mounted, it will have a defined focal point. It also can be mounted on a wall or on the underside of a permanent room object, such as a cabinet or shelf.

- *Natural lighting* is introduced into a room through windows, skylights and doors. It is difficult to control, but it is mostly agreed that a reasonable goal is to invite as much natural light into a room as possible.

Upgrading the lighting in a converted garage normally involves making improvements to all three light sources. You can do this by adding or relocating fixtures, changing the bulb types in existing fixtures, and enlarging or adding windows and skylights.

Choosing the best lights for your garage renovation comes down to basically the same choices as for any room inside the house. Bulb options include the traditional incandescent bulb, compact fluorescent bulbs, and LED bulbs. Light tubes for shoplight fixtures include traditional fluorescent tube and newer LED tubes, which you can install in a new, dedicated LED fixture or use to replace the fluorescent tubes in an existing fixture (not a simple one-for-one job).

The primary light source is the most important in a garage. Switch-controlled and mounted on the ceiling, it is the starting point for your lighting plan. Consider it carefully regardless of your intentions for how to use the garage space.

LED tubes (shown above) are very energy efficient (see page 91).

This single LED fixture casts bright, even light throughout the garage while casting minimal shadows.

Incandescent   Compact fluorescent   LED bulb

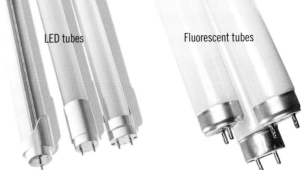

LED tubes   Fluorescent tubes

GARAGE LIGHTING QUESTIONS

Overhead light fixtures, usually called shop lights, are very common in garages and you can still use them in your new garage renovation project. They are sold mostly as 24-inch or 48-inch fixtures with light tubes of corresponding length. You can mount most types directly to a ceiling or ceiling joists or suspend them from chains that are anchored above. The most inexpensive models take fluorescent tubes, but the price hike to upgrade to energy-efficient LED products is fairly minimal.

Hard-wired or plug-in? Whether they are fluorescent or LED, you can power shop lights with a cord plugged into a nearby outlet or you can hardwire them directly to your home electrical circuit. Not all that you'll find at your local building center will be able to do both. While it is faster and far easier to hang a plug-in shop light, taking the time and effort to install hardwired fixtures makes it easier to link them to a switch and avoids exposed cords between the fixture and the outlet. On the other hand, plug-in fixtures are easier to rearrange them to suit your workspace. Your only limit will be cord length and the proximity to electrical outlets.

Linkability. Often, shop lights are sold in bundles of two, four, or more fixtures. In many cases, the fixtures are linkable—you can daisy-chain them together with built-in cords so you only need to provide power to the first fixture in the sequence. Again, this can be done either with a plug-in cord or by hardwiring to a power source through an electrical box. Linkability is a good advantage if you are installing two or more fixtures to illuminate a bay or two in your garage, but the linking cords between fixtures are usually 5 feet or shorter, so you will face some limitations when creating your lighting plan.

Directional adjustability. Some of the newer garage light products on the market are designed with a base that can screw into a standard incandescent bulb light holder. The more adaptable of these feature multiple LED arrays that fan out from the base and can be adjusted to illuminate specific areas with high precision. From a light output standpoint, they are average at best, but the fact that you can aim them is a benefit.

Lighting options have changed dramatically in the past decade, and continue to reset with each passing year. Not so long ago the basic choice was simply between incandescent bulbs and fluorescent tubes. Then, compact fluorescent bulbs (CFLs) came onto the market and had an instant impact that is making incandescents obsolete. You can still find the familiar bulbs with the glowing tungsten filaments, but most consumers now recognize that their relatively high energy consumption and shorter lifespans make them an inferior choice to other, newer types.

As quickly as CFLs changed the lighting market, in garages and elsewhere in the house, they appear to be on their way out today. In fact, two of the largest CFL manufacturers are discontinuing them. The reason, of course, is the LED. Light-emitting diodes have revolutionized the home lighting category. Although the technology is not new—basically using semiconductors to convert electricity into light—the ability to create bright white light that is similar in color to natural light is the achievement that has made LED lighting applicable in the home. The success of manufacturers in manipulating the shapes of LED tubes and bulbs to conform to conventional lighting fixtures has further accelerated its acceptance by consumers.

Replacing fluorescent tubes with LEDs is an easy way to upgrade the lighting in your garage and make the space more livable. It is a relatively easy job, although it usually is not a one-for-one swap-out. The benefit is stronger, brighter light penetration with fewer shadows. LED tubes are also much more energy efficient.

How to Install a Shop Light

Standard 24-, 48-, or 96-inch shop lights are quite easy to install. The classic fluorescent fixtures are the most inexpensive and are very easy to install and maintain. Newer LED shop lights have functional performance advantages and consume less energy, but their initial cost is somewhat higher. If you choose a product that has a plug-in cord, installation is as easy as hanging a couple of chains from the ceiling or ceiling joists and plugging the unit into an outlet. A hard-wired fixture takes a little more effort, but you don't end up with a rat's nest of power cords and the lights are easier to control with a wall switch.

To install a hard-wired LED or fluorescent shop light in your garage (or basement), you'll need:

TOOLS AND MATERIALS
Step ladder
Tape measure
Stud finder
Drill/driver
Screwdriver
Cable clamp
Light fixture
Wire nuts
Electrical box
Screws

NOTE: If you are installing your shop light as a replacement for an existing overhead light, you can simply remove the old fixture and put in the new one using the existing electrical box and wire connections. If it is an all-new fixture, you'll need to tap into an electrical circuit and add a new ceiling-mounted electrical box at the installation point.

1. Prepare the new fixture by removing the knockouts in the housing to create access directly below the electrical box in the ceiling (Photo A).

2. Remove the diffuser panel to allow access to the fixture connection points.

3. Install a cable clamp in the knockout opening (Photo A).

4. Raise the fixture up against the ceiling and check where it meets the joists. Either mark locations for toggle bolts in the ceiling at the mounting hole locations in the fixture or mark the ceiling joist locations onto the fixture body and drill new mounting holes (Photo B).

5. If not, either mark the mounting holes onto the ceiling and install toggle bolts at those points or mark the joist locations on the fixture body and drill mounting holes through the metal body.

6. Attach the fixture body to the ceiling joists with power supply wires threaded through the fixture close to the wiring connections at the ballast.

Once the fixture is securely mounted (or suspended if you are hanging it with chains or wire), make the wiring connections.

7. With the power OFF, attach the bare copper ground from the supply cable to the grounding terminal on the fixture box.

8. Attach the black lead wire from the switch to the black lead from the fixture, using a wire connector (Photo C).

9. Connect the white neutral from the switch to the white wire from the fixture.

10. Tuck the wires into the connection box in the fixture.

11. Install the LED or fluorescent tube into the fixture and test (Photo D). If it works, re-install the diffuser panel.

Whether classic fluorescent or efficient LEDs, shop lights have a place in any garage or basement.

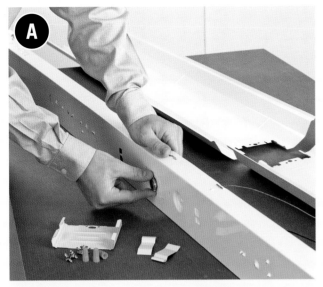

Remove the knockout in the fixture body that will align with the power source from the ceiling-mounted electrical box. Install a cable clamp in the knockout opening.

With the fixture up against the ceiling, mark toggle bolt or new mounting hole locations.

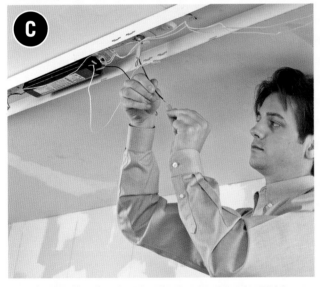

Once the fixture is fastened to the ceiling, make the wiring connections from the power source to the lead wires from the wall switch.

Install and test the tubes. Insert the diffuser panel if everything works.

How to Replace Fluorescent Tubes with LED Tubes

Removing fluorescent tube lights to replace them with LED tubes could be the last time you ever have to deal with the bulbs in your fluorescent shop light fixture.

LED light technology is evolving rapidly, with new DIY options available all the time. If your garage (or basement) features fluorescent tube light fixtures, it is easier than ever to replace the fluorescent tube with more efficient and brighter LED tubes.

While you can simply remove your fluorescent tubes, twist in LED ones, and be good to go, it's a bit more complicated than that. The one-for-one LED replacement lights work fine and are a great option for many homeowners, but they depend on the ballast in your fixture to provide power. If the ballast dies, which will happen, the lights won't work anymore. Also, the routing of the power supply through the ballast diminishes the efficiency of the LED tubes.

Getting around these limitations of the one-for-one LEDs requires a simple wiring bypass and removing the ballast. You may need to replace the sockets, often called tombstones, into which the tubes fit. As far as wiring projects go, it is about as easy as it can get.

TOOLS AND MATERIALS
LED tubes
Wire snips
Drill or screwdriver
Wire connectors

1. Shut off the power supply at the main circuit breaker panel.

2. Remove the old fluorescent tubes.

3. Remove any covers or panels that protect the wiring and the ballast in the fixture.

4. Disconnect the wires from the ballast (Photo A).

5. Snip the wires from the ballast (Photo B) and then remove the anchoring screws.

6. Discard the ballast according to your local disposal regulations—ballasts are considered toxic in many municipalities.

7. Connect the feed wires (white to white and black to black) to the wires from the bulb socket (most fixtures supply power to one end of the tube only) using wire connectors (Photo C). Make sure that you fasten the ground wire to a screw terminal in the fixture.

8. Tuck the wires out of the way, twist the LED tube into the sockets, turn on the power, and test (Photo D).

9. Replace the covers and reinstall the diffuser panel.

Unscrew the wiring connections between the ballast and the sockets.

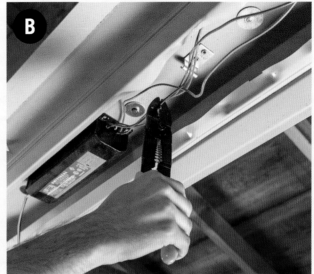

Cut the ballast wires and remove the ballast.

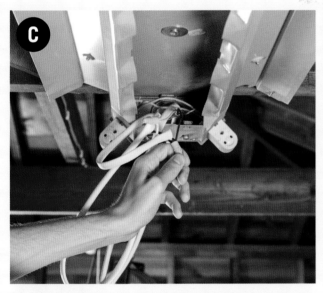

Join the feed wires (black and white) to the wires from the socket or sockets.

Twist the LED bulbs into the sockets and test. Replace the covers and diffuser.

Rehabbing a Garage Floor

If your garage renovation/repurposing plan is limited to just one project, make it the floor. Subjected to daily assaults from multi-ton vehicles, road chemicals, and constant moisture, most concrete garage floors are in pretty sad shape. Oil stains, concrete cracks and pop-outs, and just general grime take their toll. However, a vigorous cleaning, some minor repairs, and perhaps a coat or two of garage floor paint can make a huge difference, especially if you are planning to spend a significant amount of time inhabiting the space.

The first step in improving the garage floor is to repair any problems with the concrete. These can include cracks, spalling, pop-outs and divots, and moisture-related surface blemishes, just to name a few.

Few garage renovation projects can have a bigger payoff than rehabilitating a dismal floor into one that shines and is welcoming to cars and people alike.

RENT A FLOOR SCRUBBER

You can tackle very dirty and oily garage floors with an orbital floor scrubber/buffer. You can rent models, such as the 17-inch-diameter scrubber seen here, for less than $50 per day, plus scrub pads (the rental center will have both thick and thin versions). They handle much like a floor sander and it takes a little practice. Make a pass with an ammonia-based detergent, rinse, and then scrub with diluted muriatic acid. Be sure to wear protective gear and provide as much ventilation as you can.

How to Patch a Concrete Floor

As with just about any repair project, begin by cleaning the area well. Sweep, vacuum, and wash the area. For very dirty or oily floors, rent a floor scrubber (see previous page). Whether the concrete issue you face is a crack, a pop-out, or a divot, the repair procedure is basically the same.

Clear away all loose or crumbly concrete—a wire brush will get most of it (Photo A). You can also drill with a wire wheel attachment. Use a shop vac to remove all of the dust and debris. In the case of cracks, you'll need to use a cold chisel to form the edges of the crack so the walls of the void have a slight dovetail shape (Photo B). This helps prevent the concrete repair material from popping out once it cures.

You can fill minor concrete defects with concrete patching compound, which is sold as a dry powder and has very fine aggregate compared to regular concrete. This allows it to conform to small, irregular spaces more easily. Follow the instructions on the package, adding some latex bonding agent to the mix to improve elasticity and adherence. It is also a good idea to apply some bonding agent directly to the repair area immediately before you start filling in with repair compound (Photo C).

Finally, fill the crack or hole with the mixed concrete repair compound, using a drywall knife or concrete trowel. Pack the material in as tightly as you can and then trowel off the excess (Photo D). Let the repair dry overnight.

Clean out the damaged area with a wire brush and/or a wire wheel attachment in a power drill.

Use a cold chisel and mallet to taper side walls downward to help keep the repair product from popping out.

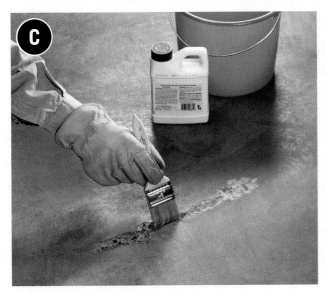

Brush a thick coat of latex binding adhesive into the repair area immediately before making the repair.

Pack the repair area with fortified concrete repair compound and then remove excess and smooth the surface with a concrete trowel.

Etching and Sealing a Concrete Floor

Did you ever wonder how concrete floors in some garages and commercial buildings get that deep color and shine? The answer is usually a combination of acid etching and sealing. Acid etching is the process of exposing the cleaned concrete to a dilute solution of muriatic acid. The concrete surface's chemical reaction with it increases its porosity and helps it absorb a finish coat.

NOTE: Instead of clear muriatic acid, you can apply acid stain, which is an acid solution that also contains a colorant. You may have to visit a concrete materials specialty store to obtain this.

Once you etch the floor with the acid solution and let it dry, you can apply a couple of coats of concrete sealer for a nice, deep finish that will darken the concrete permanently. Or, you can paint the floor with two-part epoxy garage floor paint. Do not seal if you will be painting.

A concrete floor that has been acid-etched and sealed has a lustrous, rich color and is also easier to sweep and mop than unfinished concrete.

SAFETY TIP

Muriatic acid (or any other acid that may be used on a floor) is toxic and must be handled and applied with caution. It also creates noxious fumes as it dries, so you must have good ventilation when you apply it. Wear rubber gloves, long pants and shirt, rubber boots, and a respirator when working with the acid, and take care to avoid splashing the solution onto surrounding areas. Check with your local waste department, since they may require that you remove the acid solution with a wet vac and dispose of it according to local regulations, rather than simply rinsing it off with a hose.

How to Clean and Etch a Concrete Floor

TOOLS AND MATERIALS
Muriatic acid
Mixing container
Broom or vacuum
Pump sprayer or watering can
Stiff-bristle push broom
Baking soda
Push broom

To prepare your concrete basement floor for sealing or painting, clean it well and wash it with a muriatic acid solution. Most home centers sell muriatic acid in plastic jugs. Although it is a relatively mild acid, handle it with care.

1. Prepare your acid solution. It is normally recommended that you dilute the muriatic acid at a ratio of 3 parts clean water to 1 part acid. To minimize the chance of spilling, always add water to the mixing container first and then carefully add the acid (Photo A). Set aside.

2. Sweep or vacuum the concrete floor and rinse it with clean water. The concrete should be damp, but without any puddling.

3. Spray an even coat of the solution onto the damp concrete (Photo B). A pump sprayer is a good choice, although some people prefer a plastic watering can. Work in areas small enough that the floor does not dry before you spray on the acid.

4. Use a stiff-bristle push broom to work the acid solution into the floor (Photo C). Avoid getting any ridges or broom marks in the solution, as these will bubble and foam a bit as it reacts with the concrete.

5. Let the solution stand for 5 to 10 minutes while you mix a solution of 1 cup of baking soda per 1 gallon of water (Photo D).

6. Apply the neutralizing solution. Work it in with a push broom.

7. Rinse the floor at least twice with clean water.

Add the muriatic acid to the water in the sprayer container at a rate of one part acid to three parts water.

Spay an even coat of acid solution onto the damp concrete floor.

Work the acid solution into the floor with a push broom.

Mix baking soda into water and broom it onto the floor to neutralize the acid after letting the acid work for up to 10 minutes. Rinse well with clean water.

Interiör Garage Walls

Many homeowners opt for open joist bays rather than finished interior garage walls. The open bays can be handy for some storage, such as long-handled garden tools, but they are less amenable to a home office or other habitable space—especially without insulation. Safety codes require firewall-rated wallcoverings on attached garage walls that adjoin your house; some call for fire-rated Type X drywall. If your garage is underneath inhabited space, it should have a Type X drywall ceiling, and some codes mandate a double-thick layer of drywall. You will need to tape and seal the seams on fire-rated drywall or tape them with self-adhesive firewall tape (this is not recommended if you will be painting it).

Taped drywall is probably the best choice if you plan to paint the walls, but you can certainly paint other sheet goods, including lap siding products such as shiplap, if you choose. Plywood won't be as smooth, but ¾-inch plywood will give you a solid wall for driving in nails or screws for hanging storage. For an unpainted finish that still has pattern and color, most any kind of paneling will work. If you are installing wallcoverings, it likely makes sense to add a ceiling, too.

Nicely finished interior walls create an appealing environment if you plan to spend a lot of time in your garage. Walls cut down on cleaning time by helping keep dirt and messes at bay.

SLAT-WALL STORAGE

One popular wall treatment in the garage is the slat wall. Sold in strips and in panels up to 4 × 8 feet, slat walls are quick to install, inexpensive, and they offer a host of storage options using the clips, hangers, and brackets that snap into the slats. You can also use some to hang shallow slat-wall cabinets.

Safety codes require fire-rated wallcoverings in certain areas.

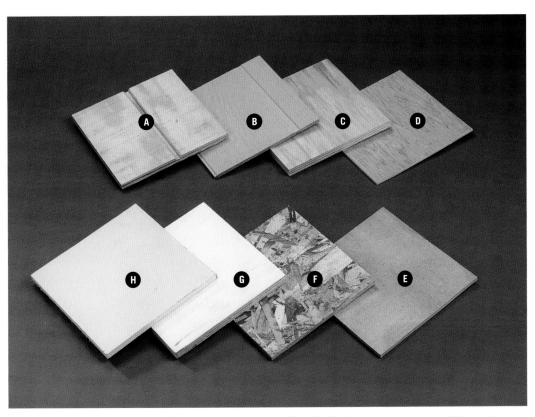

Sheet stock wallcovering options include: Exterior siding (T1-11) (A); fiber cement panels (B); interior-grade plywood (C); ¼-in.-thick floor underlayment (D); cedar siding panels (E); oriented-strand board (OSB) (F); hardwood plywood (birch is shown) (G); simple drywall (H).

How to Install Drywall in a Garage

You can select just about any type of drywall you wish for your garage walls, but do choose panels that are at least ½-inch-thick. Moisture-resistant panels are also a good idea, as garages can get pretty humid. If you plan to insulate the garage, you can install fiberglass batts or even foam panels. You can purchase either product sized for the stud bays. Depending on your climate and whether you will be heating and/or cooling the garage, local building codes may require a vapor barrier between the wall insulation and the drywall. Check with your local building department, as vapor retarders vary widely by region.

TOOLS AND MATERIALS

Drywall
Drywall lifter
1 ¼-in. drywall screws
Utility knife
Straightedge (preferably a drywall T-square)
Drywall tape (optional)
Joint compound (optional)

1. Starting in a corner, use a drywall lifter to raise a full panel to at least ½ inch above the garage floor.

2. Drive 1 ¼-inch drywall screws every 16 inches or so (Photo A).

NOTE: If you are installing drywall on the ceiling as well, panel the ceiling first and butt the wall panels up against the ceiling drywall.

3. Use a utility knife and straightedge (preferably a drywall T-square) to cut panels to fit (Photo B). Simply score along the cutting line and snap the panel. Finish the cut by slicing the paper facing.

4. If you wish to paint the walls, cover the seams with drywall tape and joint compound (Photo C) and cover the screwheads.

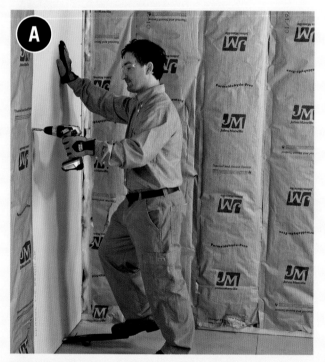

Use a drywall lifter to raise the panels off the floor as you attach them.

Use a utility knife and drywall T-square to cut drywall panels to fit.

Seal the seams between panels and at corners with drywall tape and joint compound.

How to Install Wall Sheathing in a Garage

Wall sheathing panels, such as OSB and plywood, make a durable wall that stands up to bumps from lawn mowers or bicycles. You can conceal the seams between panels with thin molding strips, such as screen retainer strips or low-profile T-molding.

TOOLS AND MATERIALS
Wall sheathing panels
Construction adhesive
1⅝-inch self-tapping drywall or deck screws
Jig saw
Molding strips (optional)
Long-handed roller (optional)
Light-colored paint (optional)

1. Starting in a corner, add a bead of construction adhesive on the face of each wall stud and put a full panel in place. The adhesive will stabilize the wall and limit rattling.

2. Secure each panel with self-tapping, 1⅝-inch drywall or deck screws (Photo A). Leave a slight gap between panels and keep panel edges midway across wall studs.

3. Use a jig saw to make cutouts for electrical boxes (Photo B). If you wish, you can conceal the seams between panels with thin, narrow molding strips (Photo C).

4. If you choose to paint the walls, use a long-handled roller and select a lighter colored paint.

Begin installing the sheathing panels at a corner, lifting the panels so they do not contact the floor directly. Attach the panels with screws so the panel edges fall midway across wall studs.

Use a jigsaw to make cutouts in the panel for electrical boxes.

Tack thin strips of molding over the seams between sheathing panels.

Garage Windows and Skylights

Plenty of garages have windows, even if they are only part of the garage door. But most often, they are small, horizontal hopper-style windows that offer little ambient light. If you plan to spend some serious time in a garage room, consider upgrading the windows or perhaps even adding a skylight. In both cases, look for an operable window unit. Garages can get quite musty and you'll appreciate the fresh air.

Replacing a small hopper-style garage window with a deeper model, or simply adding a window where there was none, brings high-quality (and free) illumination into your garage. And why not add a skylight in addition to or instead of a garage window?

Installing a Garage Window

Window framing is done essentially the same way in a garage as elsewhere in your house. You'll need to remove any wallcoverings in the project area and then install studs, a sill, and header to create the rough opening.

After marking the corners of the cutout on the interior side, use a reciprocating saw to cut out the siding in the installation area.

After flashing the rough opening, set the new window in the opening so it is level and centered. Nail it in place and install trim on the exterior and interior.

Installing a Garage Skylight

Frame for the skylight on the interior and mark the corners of the opening. Cut out the roof section from above using a circular saw. Tack a board onto the waste section before cutting all the way through to prevent it from falling down into the garage.

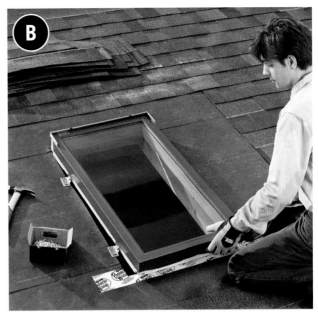

Remove the shingles in the installation area then install self-adhesive flashing around the opening. Set the window unit in place and fasten it to the roof deck.

Add more flashing around the skylight curb. Install the top flashing last so all flashing strips overlap from above.

Install the flashing kit, reserving the head flashing for last. Reinstall shingles up to the skylight curb.

Making a Shed Habitable

The search for space can lead down some interesting paths, including those in the garden—provided that path leads to a shed. These outbuildings have pluses and minuses as living spaces. If your biggest need for a home office is some peace and quiet, a shed, especially a remote one, can provide it. If your home-based job or hobby can get messy, setting up in a shed is a good way to keep the mess out of the house.

Since sheds typically are uninsulated, have little or no ventilation, and may well have a dirt or gravel floor, your basic backyard shed will normally require some upgrades if your plan is to spend a significant amount of time in it. Plus, a shed with no wall or ceiling insulation is probably going to be quite loud inside, as will any shed with metal-panel walls or roof. Security also can be an issue if you plan to store any valuable machinery, supplies, or equipment there.

This shed demonstrates how good design choices transform an outbuilding into a livable, pleasing space.

Shed Requirements

Whether your current shed has the capacity to take on inhabitants and new functions is largely a matter of size, although other factors are also important. If you are building a new shed or having one built, you have the luxury of planning the structure to accommodate your needs, both current and future. Variables include location, size, shape, building materials, window quantity, door style, and amenities, such as wiring or plumbing.

Size:
Small: 4 × 6 to 6 × 8 feet
Medium: 6 × 10 to 8 × 12 feet
Large: 8 × 16, 10 × 12, 12 × 16 feet

Shape/roofline options:
Shed, gable, saltbox, gambrel (barn)

Wall and Roof Materials:
Wood sheathing: plywood, oriented strand board, siding panels, shiplap
Metal: shed kit panels, corrugated roof panels
Vinyl/Plastic: lap siding, pre-fab sheds, shed kits

Foundation:
Wood/timber: timbers, treated lumber frame, wood posts
Concrete slab: poured concrete 4 to 6 inches thick
Concrete footings: tube formed below grade
Piers: precast concrete set on a gravel drainage base

Anyone can construct a simple kit shed for storage. Throw in some creativity and you can have an appealing office or personal space. *Photo by Rebecca Ittner*

Getting Power to a Shed

For an existing shed or other outbuilding to have significant value as a habitable space, you'll need power. Whether your plan is to convert it to a home office, craft or arts studio, or fun outdoor bar, you'll have much more success if it has permanent lighting and a place to plug in the necessary equipment.

The easiest solution is to run a new electrical circuit from an empty slot and a new circuit breaker in your main service panel. Whether you can do this easily or not depends on the excess capacity of your panel and, to a lesser extent, the distance from the panel to the structure. From the panel, wires travel (usually through rigid conduit) to an exit point, typically in the rim joist of your house and located as close possible to the outbuilding. The conduit and wire connect to a waterproof L-body fitting mounted on the exterior wall and then are directed below

ground through exterior-rated conduit containing outdoor-rated UF cable. At a depth of 12 to 24 inches, the cable runs through a trench to the structure, where a sweep and conduit direct the wire up to the desired height on the exterior of the outbuilding wall. There, a connection is made either to another L-body or, more likely, to an outdoor box containing a GFCI-protected receptacle. From this box the cable feeds into the structure and routes to the planned receptacle, switch, and fixture boxes. Success as a DIY project also depends on your experience and your confidence in doing home wiring work. As such projects go, running a new circuit to an outbuilding is an intermediate to advanced skill level undertaking. It takes a lot of time and requires a permit, but it could save you thousands of dollars versus hiring a professional electrician.

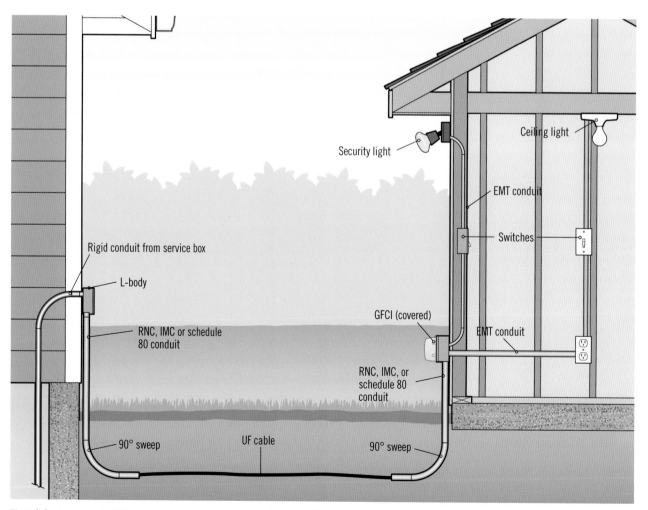

Electricity for an outbuilding requires wiring a new circuit starting in an empty slot in your main electrical service panel into your yard.

If you have a very large shed or outbuilding and you will need more than one circuit, or perhaps a 240-volt circuit for equipment such as an arc welder or sauna stove, the solution is to install a subpanel in the outbuilding. A double-pole breaker in the main panel draws current from both hot "bus bars" in the panel to feed the subpanels, which are generally 30 to 50 amps. Installing one still requires that the subpanel does not overtax the electrical draw limits in your main panel. The primary advantage to a subpanel is that you can install breakers for multiple circuits inside of it, meaning you do not have to fill up all of the often-scarce breaker slots in the main panel. This is an even more ambitious project than simply running a single new circuit and in most cases is best left to a professional.

How Power Gets from Your House to Your Shed

Cable from a new breaker in the main service panel runs to an electrical junction box near the point where rigid conduit runs to the exterior, usually through a hole drilled into the rim joist.

Exterior-rated conduit attaches to an L-body fitting mounted on the house exterior (inset photo), then runs downward to a depth of 12 to 24 inches and attaches to a 90° sweep.

From the L-body fitting, UF cable travels through a trench to reach the outbuilding. The cable should be contiguous, with no splices.

At the shed, a sweep and conduit direct the UF cable upward to reach an outdoor connection box, often containing a protected GFCI receptacle. The UF cable feeds the connection in the box, where conduit directs power into the structure and distributes it throughout to individual switches, receptacles, and fixtures.

Shed Lighting

How you choose to set up your artificial lighting scheme depends, of course, on the intended use of your shed. Presumably, you'll have at least one window to introduce natural light. If not, you should add one, and the process is fundamentally the same as adding a garage window (see page 104). If you are planning to have a workstation, you'll appreciate having a nearby window to stare out for inspiration. For ventilation purposes, an operable window is best.

If your shed does have power and lighting already, the light is very likely a single-bulb fixture mounted on the wall or the middle of the ceiling. This is better than nothing, but it will cast shadowy, nondirected light that is not ideal for most purposes. Consider tapping into a switch-activated overhead bulb fixture by adding another light to the chain. A wall-mounted light or even a pendant light located near your intended work area is a good bet. Or, you can simplify things by adding a small shop light (LED is best) that plugs into a wall outlet and requires no wiring.

If you are adding power to your shed (see page 108), consider your needs for both light locations and outlet locations. A single overhead light might be all you need, but, because headroom is usually lower in a shed, choose a fixture with a protective cage over the bulb. In most cases, outlets in a shed will be easiest to access if they are mounted 36 to 48 inches up from the floor (standard wall switch height). If you are installing a wall switch, locate it just inside the door.

If your shed has exposed wall studs and you do not plan to add interior walls, you'll need to run your new light and power circuits through conduit to protect the cables.

TIPS FOR ADDING NEW LIGHT AND POWER CIRCUITS IN A SHED

Photo A. Decide where you want the lights, outlets, and switches to be located and start by installing the boxes for these system components. Use circular ceiling light boxes. Many find it easier to hook up the conduit or connector fitting that connects directly to the box before attaching the box to the rafters or studs. Use set-screw fittings or offset fittings to connect the conduit to the boxes. **TIP:** If you are installing an overhead light fixture in a gable-roof shed with open rafters, add a cross block between two opposite rafters to create a flat installation area for mounting the ceiling box.

Photo B. Install conduit, boxes, and fittings for the entire run, from the service entry point (usually a junction box or receptacle box) to the other outlet, fixture, and switch boxes. Remove the cover plates from elbow fittings, then fish lengths of THNN hot (black), neutral (white), and ground (green) wires (do not used sheathed cable) from point to point in the layout, leaving at least 8 inches of wire protruding from each box. **TIP:** Bind the ends of the wires for each run with electrical tape to make it easier to fish them through the conduit (inset photo).

Photo C. Attach the wire leads to the receptacles, switches, and light fixtures. Tuck the capped wires neatly into the boxes and attach the devices to the boxes. With the power off at the main breaker, make the hookups to the new breaker at the main electrical service panel. Turn on power and test the circuit and devices.

Shed Walls and Ceilings

Wall and ceiling coverings are not required—and usually are absent—in a shed, even one that has been rehabbed into a living space. But they give the space a more finished appearance that feels more like a room and allows you to relax or work in a more pleasant environment. They also hide the wall studs, insulation, and any wiring in the wall cavities. If your studs, rafters, and wall and roof sheathing are in good condition and installed neatly, you can paint them for a "room" feel and get creative with using the stud cavities for storage and display.

As with a garage or basement, you can choose sheet goods or planks for the wallcoverings and the ceiling. Drywall is not a good choice for a shed or a rustic outbuilding as it is too susceptible to moisture damage and is less durable in a frequently used space. Cedar or pine tongue-and-groove planks, sometimes called shiplap, are a warm, decorative product for finishing the interior of your shed office. Use matching dimensional lumber to make trim boards for a more finished look. A coat of wood stain or topcoat will protect the wood, deepen its color, and make it easier to clean.

Consider ceiling height when you determine whether to include a ceiling in your shed. Paneling fastened directly to the rafters will encroach into the ceiling height by only a quarter inch or so, but thicker material will take a bigger bite. Some taller sheds can handle a drop ceiling—usually cross braces between rafters that support a sheet-goods "floor" for a storage area.

Wood planks, such as shiplap, add warmth to shed space.

If you are insulating your walls and ceilings, install wallcoverings to conceal and protect the insulation.

Shed walls and ceilings do not require wall coverings to look homey and function practically. Cross blocks and shelving between two rafters at the end of a gable roof add some handy storage.

Shed Ventilation

Ventilation likely will be an issue in converting any outbuilding into living space. If your shed has an operable window and a door you can leave ajar, you have a good starting point. A plug-in fan that directs stagnant air out through those openings is a simple and flexible way to add airflow, while a large, high-end shed with a gable or cathedral roof is a candidate for a ceiling fan.

Many sheds have open rafters with either a vented soffit or mesh-covered eaves on the exterior to allow hot air to flow out of the shed. Roof vents, even passive ones, can aid this flow. Spinning turbine vents move more air than a simple exhaust vent, and a solar-powered version is a good choice that requires no electrical hookup. In a similar but more focused vein, a wall-mounted vent fan is a simple solution for providing needed ventilation and airflow exactly where you want it. You simply drill a hole through the wall, attach the fan mechanism, provide a vent opening cover on the exterior side, and plug it in. Hard-wired models are most common.

 SHED VENTILATION OPTIONS

Roof vents, even passive ones such as this familiar vent that exhausts an attic, give air a route out of your shed.

A ceiling fan in a shed with plenty of headroom assists air movement and provides an elegant design surprise for an outbuilding.

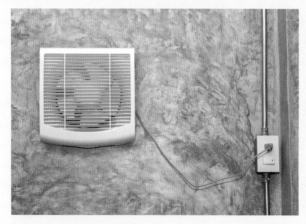

This wall-mounted vent fan is a switched outlet integrated into the conduit electrical supply system.

You can also set a fan near your workspace and point it right at yourself, which, while it won't improve ventilation, at least can make you feel cooler.

Shed Heating and Cooling

Maintaining a comfortable environment in your shed office or other habitable outbuilding inevitably involves heating and cooling. Unless you're investing in a large (200 square feet or more) outbuilding designed from the get-go to be lived in, you probably don't want to pay for a full-blown HVAC system. But as long as your shed has power, you can at least extend its seasonal usability with just the supplemental heating and cooling appliances you may already have inside your home.

Short of installing a full heat plant, the primary heating options for an office shed include electric space heaters and baseboard heaters. In both cases, the ideal output is easiest to determine based on the shed's square footage. The space heater will have its wattage as well as coverage in square footage listed on the packaging and probably the unit itself. Popular, easy-to-find types include infrared, fan, radiant, and ceramic. Some are freestanding and portable, others are wall-mounted. Baseboard heaters can be a bit trickier, but the standard guide is that your heater should output 10 watts per square foot. The most efficient baseboard heaters are hardwired. Some include an integral thermostat; others are wired through a wall-mounted thermostat that can control multiple lengths of heater. Some models simply plug in to a wall outlet.

Cooling options for a shed include window air conditioners, through-the-wall air conditioners, and portable air conditioners—often on wheels and usually vented with flexible ductwork meant to be exhausted through an insert panel that fits in a window.

An assortment of electric space heaters are available for providing season-extending heat to your shed office.

DUCTLESS MINI-SPLIT SYSTEMS

A relative newcomer in the home HVAC world, ductless mini-split systems that provide cooling—or both heating and cooling—to garages, outbuildings, and even interior rooms with underserved environmental demands are becoming more popular. These systems are called "split" because they split the parts of an AC system in to two units. One, an air handler, is bracket-mounted to an interior wall and contains sensors, controls, and basically the brains of the system. The other part, installed outdoors, is similar in look and function to a central air conditioning condenser unit. Wires and refrigerant and condensation lines connect the two parts through a 3 to 4 inch hole in the wall.

Most mini-split systems will easily cool a shed up to 200 square feet. Units that contain a heat pump can warm the room, as well. They are low profile and very convenient. Lower-end models start at around $1,000 and the prices go up quickly from there.

A ductless mini-split system comprises an outdoor component (left) that does most of the work and an indoor, wall-mounted air handler (right) that controls everything.

Shed Floors

Most sheds, including shed kits or prebuilt sheds, have a plywood floor. Some, however, are built directly onto a concrete pad. Others may have loose rock, pavers, or even dirt floors—none of which are great choices for an office shed or other inhabitable outbuilding. Whatever your current floor, it is almost certain than paying some attention to what is below your feet will have high payback in your shed renovation project.

The types of floorcoverings that are suitable for a shed are pretty much the same as for garages (page 98) and basements (page 65). The main attributes to look for are moisture resistance, durability, and cleanability. But in a shed that you are trying to present visually as a living space, charm and warmth are also important considerations. Because you'll be working or pacing

Vinyl plank flooring is easy to install, has anti-fatigue properties, resists moisture, and comes in an array of colors and surprisingly convincing "faux" styles.

around on it, shock absorption comes into play, as does thickness. In most sheds, you'll want to subtract as little as possible from the total headroom when choosing a flooring product. Given all these considerations, you can't go wrong with vinyl or paint.

Vinyl

Traditionally, vinyl flooring has come in two types: sheet vinyl and vinyl tile. Both can work very well in a shed and both are relatively inexpensive and easy to install. Some vinyl tiles need to be set into adhesive, while others, usually called stickybacks, have a peelable paper backing that, once removed, lets you press the self-adhesive back tile into place directly on the subfloor or underlayment. A more recent product type in the vinyl world is plank flooring. These rigid tongue-and-grooved planks are highly resistant to moisture, come in a wide variety of styles, snap together easily so are simple to install, and feel warm and slightly soft underfoot.

Paint

You can't get much thinner than paint when it comes to floors, so a painted floor definitely makes sense in a shed office with a low ceiling. Give the plywood a good washing and maybe a sanding for good measure before applying color. You can paint in one solid color or create a fun pattern. If you use a hard, glossy paint, such as porch enamel, the surface will hold up very well and be easy to keep clean.

If your shed has a plywood floor, as most do, you don't need to add new floorcoverings to spruce things up. You can even get creative, as with the faux-brick floor shown here.
Photo by Rebecca Ittner

SHED KITS AND CUSTOM SHEDS

The sudden interest in office sheds and other kinds of livable outdoor structures resulting from the shift to working at home has bolstered the market for shed kits and custom sheds. Some are shipped in flat packs for assembly and others are shipped fully assembled for contractors to install and hook up. These are not the most inexpensive options, but if you want a great office shed in a hurry and with little hard work on your part, they're are good candidates.

A well-designed and positioned custom barrier defines where living spaces end and working spaces begin while contributing positively to a room's overall visual impact.
Photo by Tracy Ong

Section 3: Easy DIY Projects for the Hardworking Home

Privacy Barriers and Room Dividers

For many years realtors, house designers, and homebuyers have extolled the virtues of open floor plans and open concept home design. Home renovations have centered on removing walls and the creation of "great rooms." Being able to see all the way from the front door to the back of the house has been a goal. Since the sudden move to home officing and home schooling however, the trend toward openness is reversing itself rapidly and the walls suddenly are going back up. Or, if not walls, then privacy barriers and room dividers.

Dividing space is a key objective when setting up any room for multiple users to participate in home office work or distance learning. You also may choose to create spatial separation in order to have a visual and psychological reminder of the importance of segregating work life from home life. In the majority of cases, temporary or portable barriers are more practical than permanent ones, and they certainly make more sense for renters or short-term occupants. On the other hand, creating permanent room dividers or even reapportioning space with partition walls are options that can offer a greater range of design possibilities, more privacy, and better sound control. If you are a homeowner and expect to maintain your living situation for some time, it may be worth

A simple freestanding bookcase, or even a floor-to-ceiling built-in, creates visual separation and valuable storage space.

Adding ceiling-mounted or freestanding textiles temporarily cordons off space with a neutral background for video conferencing without creating a sterile feel.

Doors, such as the multi-pane French doors in a sliding barn door configuration, can separate out spare space in any room, large or small.

investing in more lasting and ultimately more gratifying improvements.

Reasons for adding a room divider or privacy barrier:

- Separating two or more workspaces

- Isolating workspaces and living areas

- Creating a sound barrier for privacy

- Allowing you to "close the door" when you are done working

Here are a few examples of strategies you can use to subdivide floorspace, temporarily or permanently, in a room.

- Make or purchase a folding panel-style room divider to place between work areas as needed.

- Create smaller privacy screens that rest between users on a long, shared worksurface.

- Hang draperies or textiles, including on freestanding racks or structures, to temporarily close off a work area, dampen noise, or provide a suitable video background.

- Build a kneewall to create visual separation for a work area.

- Build a partition wall with a door to close off a portion of a larger room.

- Add doors, such as sliding barn doors or French doors, to cordon off a foyer or anteroom.

- Build a floor-to-ceiling bookcase, space-dividing shelving unit, or another architectural element to separate a space and add storage.

Folding Room Dividers

Various cultures have used the classic, multi-panel room divider for decorative and functional purposes since the 200s BCE in China. Made of at least three tall, vertical pieces connected with hinges, it supports itself when placed in a zigzag configuration. Furniture, import, and online stores carry a vast array of styles, from Victorian to Asian to Contemporary. Easy to adjust and store, they are an ideal option for temporarily creating small rooms in a big room. You can buy room dividers and privacy screens—you'll find a wealth of beautiful options in a wide range of prices. Or, you can build your own.

The collapsible nature of trifold, freestanding room dividers makes them quick and convenient to use.

TYPES OF FREESTANDING, FOLDING ROOM DIVIDERS

DIY louvered screen. Connect three 24-in. or wider louvered closet doors with butt or bifold hinges for a simple, inexpensive folding screen. Stain or paint to your preferences. Tip: Look for models that are not predrilled for hardware.

Wood and fabric. Stretch and secure decorative fabric over the openings of wood frames for a fun design option with relatively little work. Tip: Fabric that is printed on both sides yields a more versatile result.

Online. With a quick internet search, you can find unique room divider screens to fit any budget or aesthetic, from simple to ornate.

Readymade Folding Room Divider

The simplest solution is to find three or more louvered closet doors and connect them with butt hinges or bifold door hinges and then paint or stain them. But if you are feeling a bit more ambitious, take a tour of the millwork section in your local building center and see what your creativity can conjure. The room divider shown here is fabricated with stock maple moldings, maple cabinet doors, and light diffuser panels (sold in 2 × 4-foot panels) for fluorescent light fixtures.

Fabricated from stock moldings, cabinet doors, and fluorescent light diffuser panels, this handsome room divider requires minimal cutting to build, but careful placement of fasteners has a big payoff.

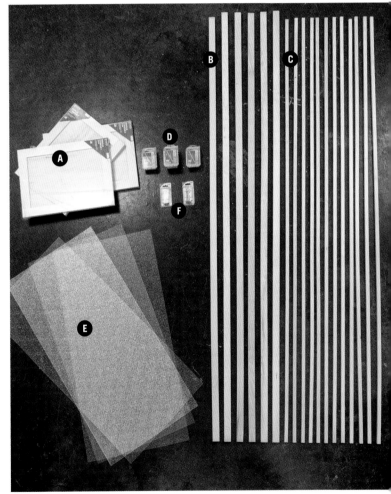

The room divider shown here requires the following materials: (A) Three ¾ x 16 x 21½-in. framed maple cabinet doors; (B) Six 1¹⁄₁₆ x 1½ x 96-in. maple; (C) Ten ½ x ¾ x 96-in. maple stop molding; (D) #8 x 1½-in. GRK screws and 1-in. brads; (E) Three ¹⁄₁₆ x 24 x 48-in. light diffuser panels; Clear silicone adhesive.

READYMADE ROOM DIVIDER

CUTLIST

KEY	QTY	PART NAME	DIMENSION	MATERIAL
A	6	Upright	$^{11}/_{16} \times 1\frac{1}{2} \times 64"$	Maple
B	9	Rails	$^{11}/_{16} \times 1\frac{1}{2} \times 21\frac{1}{2}"$	Maple
C	12	Retainer (horiz)	$\frac{1}{2} \times \frac{3}{4} \times 21\frac{1}{2}"$	Maple
D	18	Retainer (vert)	$\frac{1}{2} \times \frac{3}{4} \times 11^{9}/_{16}"$	Maple
E	3	Diffuser lite	$^{1}/_{16} \times 21 \times 38"$	Acrylic

TOOLS AND MATERIALS

Tape measure

(10) $\frac{1}{2} \times \frac{3}{4} \times 96$-in. maple stop molding

(3) $\frac{3}{4} \times 16 \times 21\frac{1}{2}$-in. framed maple cabinet doors

(6) $^{11}/_{16} \times 1\frac{1}{2} \times 96$-in. maple

Wood glue

Clamps

Square

Drill

#8 × 1½-in. GRK screws

$^{3}/_{16}$-inch-thick shims

Spacers

Brads (1 inch, 1½-inch)

Straightedge

Utility knife

(3) $^{1}/_{16} \times 24 \times 48$-inch light diffuser panels

Clear silicone adhesive

4 butt or bi-fold hinges

Eye protection

Ear protection

Gloves

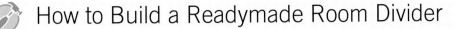

How to Build a Readymade Room Divider

Larger building centers and some lumber yards have a large selection of in-stock wood moldings, such as the ones used here to make this room divider. If your local store does not carry them, ask at the lumber desk as they will likely be able to order them for you. The basic idea with this room divider is to capture a light diffuser panel (clear or translucent) within a frame made from stock maple molding and a frame-and-panel maple cabinet door occupying the bottom quarter of each panel. You'll need at least three panels so the final project will be freestanding when the panels are hinged together, but you can add as many panels as you wish if you want it to have a longer footprint.

Tip: For perfectly symmetrical panels, gang-cut all of the same-sized parts (including the rails, uprights, and retainers) before beginning assembly.

1. Place 3 rails between each pair of uprights 8 inches and 17½ inches up from the bottom (measured to the bottom faces of the rails).

2. Apply wood glue at the joints and then clamp each assembly. Check for square.

3. Drill pilot holes as symmetrical as possible from joint to joint, then drive a pair of screws through each joint (Photo A).

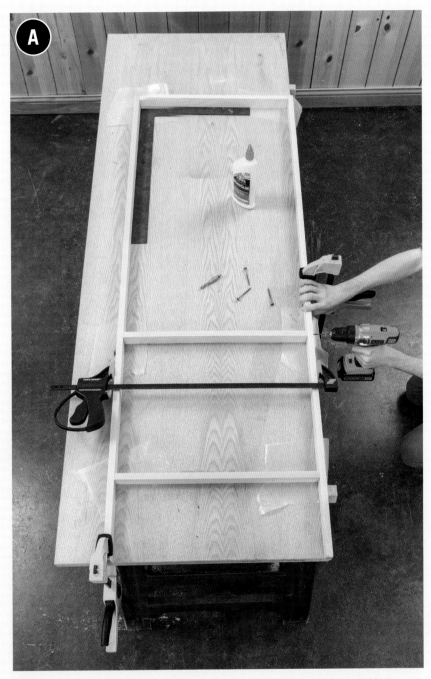

Capture the rails between the uprights by driving two screws, evenly spaced, at each joint.

4. Attach the horizontal and vertical retainer strips on one side of the panel frame to create a complete frame within each frame opening.

5. Attach the retainers to the rails and uprights, making sure to set the outer faces of the retainers back ³⁄₁₆ inch from the outside of the frame. The shims will be a big help here.

6. Drill pilot holes and drive 1 screw through the upright to attach the intermediate horizontal retainers.

7. Drill pilot holes and drive 1-inch brads to attach the top and bottom retainers to the rails.

8. Insert the vertical retainers between the horizontal retainers.

9. Drill pilot holes and attach the retainers to the uprights with brads (Photo B). Keep the retainer faces.

10. Score the acrylic diffuser panels to size for each frame opening using a straightedge and a utility knife. Snap the pieces as you would when cutting drywall. These 2 × 4-foot panels are cut down to 21 × 38 inches.

11. Lay each assembly flat with the open side of the frames facing up and apply a thin bead of silicone adhesive around each frame opening.

12. Set a cut acrylic panel into each opening (Photo C and inset).

13. Flip each assembly over and attach the horizontal and vertical retainers to capture the acrylic panels, using the same attachment scheme as for the other side of each frame opening.

Drive pilot holes for all screws and brads, including those attaching the vertical retainers to the uprights.

Apply a thin bead of silicone adhesive around each opening to make a setting base. Place the acrylic panel into each opening (inset).

14. Center a cabinet door in each of the bottom frame openings, using spacers to keep the spacing even (Photo D).

15. Drill pilot holes and drive 1 or 1½-inch brads through the uprights and bottom rail into the cabinet door frame.

16. Connect the panels with hinges (Photo E). This screen has one 7 inches down from the top and 10 inches up from the bottom.

17. Finish the room divider as you wish or leave it plain. The wood parts here have a light coat of UV-resistant sealant.

With even spacing, set a door panel into each bottom frame opening. Attach the doors by driving brads through the uprights and the bottom rail.

Fasten the room divider panels together with butt or bifold hinges (shown). Apply a topcoat to the wood parts if you wish.

Woven Room Divider

The room divider in this project is lightweight and easy to move around, yet still durable and stylish. Strips of ¼-inch-thick plywood make up the woven infill of the three cedar frame panels. Unfortunately, the lauan (also called luan) plywood from which the version seen here is made has become very scarce in recent years owing to overharvesting. But you can achieve the basic look and use the construction techniques with other, more available ¼-inch sheet stock or paneling.

As shown, the overall dimensions for each panel are 72 inches high by 3½ inches deep by 24 inches wide. Because of the relatively wide 1 × 4 stock used to make the frames you could make a two-panel version that would be reasonably stable, but for better stability and more coverage three or more panels is recommended.

For each panel you build you'll need three 1 × 4" x 8' pieces of 1 x 4 (cedar or clear pine); three ¾ × ¾" × 8 ft. strips of matching cove or quarter-round molding; and one 4 × 4 ft. piece of ¼"-thick sheet stock.

An open grid of cedar blocking provides visual relief at the top of each panel of this room divider.

How to Build a Woven Room Divider

1. Lay out reference marks on the legs at 10 ¼ inches and 48 ¼ inches, with the middle stretchers in the top spaced 3½ inches apart. It's best to lay the legs next to one another on the flat and gang-mark the reference lines (Photo A)

2. Attach the stretchers between the legs at the reference lines using glue and countersunk 2-inch screws.

3. Lay the vertical slats on a flat worksurface and weave the horizontal slats through them to create a woven panel with final size of 22½ × 48 inches (Photo B).

4. Fasten retainers inside the panel opening on the frame so the inside of the retainer frame is 1½ inches from the edges of the legs.

5. Fasten the retainer strips with finish or brad nails (Photo C).

6. Lay the assembly flat and set the woven panel onto the retainer frame. Install another retainer frame on the other side of the panel to secure it.

7. Install the vertical dividers for the grid on top. The fit between the upper stretchers should be tight enough to friction-fit them in place, but you also can secure them by driving brads or finish nails at an angle through the stretcher edges and into the dividers.

8. Separate the completed panels with a spacer the same thickness of the hinge barrel and clamp them together. Attach the hinges (Photo D).

9. Fill the screw counterbores and finish as desired.

Gang the legs together with the ends flush and use a combination square to mark reference lines for the stretchers.

Weave together the horizontal and vertical slats. No additional fastening is required, but be gentle when you move the woven panel into the frame.

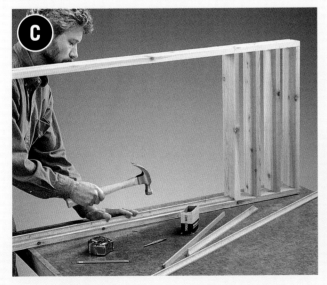

Install a retainer frame inside the panel frame opening.

Connect your panels together with butt hinges

Kneewalls

For a more permanent home addition that provides visual separation but doesn't shrink the space as much as a large room divider or partition wall, build a small kneewall, also known as a stub wall or half-wall. This is a short, open-topped partition wall that allows you to divide space without impacting the room's openness. Add a cap board to the kneewall and use it to display plants or other objects and increase the visual separation in a changeable way.

You can add an outlet to a kneewall for additional electrical access in the work area. The wiring work should of course be done before you install the kneewall and will likely require a permit and on-site inspection.

You should secure a kneewall to the floor and an adjoining wall at an edge of the work area you want to create. You can build it to match the paint and trim of the room, or create a fun and contrasting design.

Build your kneewall as an echo or complement to the overall design of the room.

The interior of a kneewall resembles that of any other partition wall (see page 132), except that it is not anchored from above. Consequently, it is important to secure wall framing to the existing floor and wall framing very well. Aligning the wall with existing joists and wall studs will save you some time and effort. However, you can position it just about anywhere if you cut into the wall or floor and install blocking within a frame opening to secure the kneewall framing.

This unassuming kneewall project serves its purpose and is unobtrusive.

Building a Kneewall

This project shows you how to build a permanent kneewall in a typical living area using the same wall and trim styles as the rest of the room. The room itself has wall-to-wall carpeting and typical drywall. It requires cutting into the wallcovering to create access for attaching the kneewall framing to the wall studs. You'll need to cut into the drywall to reveal a complete wall framing opening and install blocking between the studs to anchor the kneewall (see previous page). Remove the drywall to reveal half of each wall stud so you will have a nailing surface for patching the wall when the project is done. If you align your kneewall

with wall studs, you could conceivably attach the framing to the studs without cutting out the drywall.

It is best to remove floorcovering, such as carpet, within the kneewall area and attach the wall base plate directly to the floor sheathing. In most cases it should be possible to locate at least one or two floor joists below the floor sheathing for anchoring the base plate securely. Simply attaching the base plate to the sheathing will result in a less secure connection, which can be problematic, since there is to support from above.

How to Build a Kneewall

TOOLS AND MATERIALS

Pencil	Level	Drywall compound
Measuring tape	Tacks	Paint
Stud finder (optional)	Construction screws	Trim
Drywall saw	Wiring (optional)	Brads or finish nails
Saw	Outlet (optional)	Cap plate
Prybar	Drywall screws or nails	Eye protection
Masking tape		Ear protection
Utility knife	Metal corner bead	Gloves
Construction adhesive	Saw	
Square	Drywall tape	

1. Shut off electrical power at the main service panel.

2. Mark the wall stud locations within or near the project area and remove all wall coverings as necessary to gain access to the studs.

3. Carefully remove any wall base trim in the installation area and mark out the wall location area on the floorcovering with masking tape. If you want the kneewall to have the same base trim treatment, you'll probably need to remove the floorcovering in the installation area. This is particularly true of carpet and carpet pad. Cut and remove the floorcovering and any tack strips at the wall (Photo A). Remove all debris from the installation area.

4. Assemble the frame (Photo B). In most cases, it's easiest to build the kneewall frame completely before you install it—you can even build it in a workshop if it's small enough to move to the installation area. A simple 2 × 4 frame with 16-inch on-center should suffice. Make sure the top and bottom plates are the same length.

5. Position the 2 × 4 frame in the installation area to make sure it fits as you planned.

6. Remove the wall frame, lay a bead of construction adhesive on the floor sheathing, and then replace the wall frame.

7. Check that everything is square and then tack the wall frame to the sheathing and the wall stud or blocking.

8. Attach the frame to the wall and floor with constructions screws, driving into wall studs or blocking and into joists where possible (Photo C). If you are planning a new outlet, install wiring (or have it installed) at this point.

Remove old floorcoverings in the exact installation area to expose the floor sheathing.

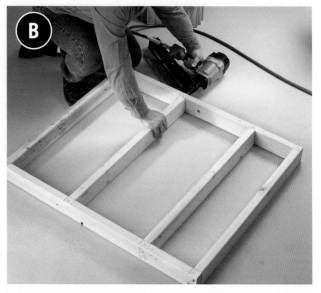

Build the kneewall frame by attaching the frame studs to the top and bottom plates.

Attach the kneewall frame in the installation area with construction adhesive and screws driven at stud, joist, and blocking locations.

Install the wall surfaces and patch at the adjoining point as needed.

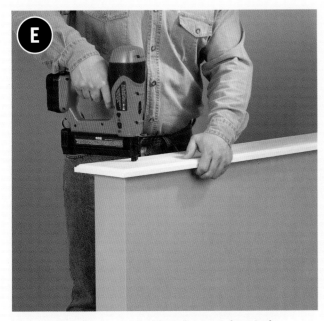

You may also want to cut and install some mitered trim moldings between the cap bottom and walls for a more refined appearance.

Replace the original base moldings and attach new base moldings to the kneewall.

9. Cut drywall to fit each side of the wall and attach it with drywall screws or nails.

10. Cut metal corner bead for the outside corners and install them, as well (Photo D).

11. Patch the adjoining wall surface as needed. Install vertical wall blocking if the wall patches need a sturdy nailing surface. Finish the wall and any patches with drywall tape and compound.

12. Paint the kneewall and patch areas.

13. Install trim using brads or finish nails.

14. Attach the cap plate with brads or finish nails to protect the fragile drywall (Photo E). One that echoes the base trim profiles and overhangs the kneewall an equal amount on all side works well.

15. Cut matching base trim to fit and install it on the kneewall (Photo F). The new trim should conceal the area where the old floorcovering meets the wall.

Partition Walls

The ultimate solution to creating permanent, separate space (short of building an addition) is to build a partition wall with a door. A full-width, floor-to-ceiling partition wall can convert one large room into two smaller ones with distinct functions and privacy. Creating an all-new room offers many advantages that may outweigh the loss of open space, especially if the room being divided is underused or larger than is needed. For example, if your 300-square-foot basement family room saw a lot of use when the kids were young but you now only use a sectional in the corner to watch TV, why not convert a third or even half of it to a permanent home office?

As with kneewalls, you'll need to consider how to manage the floorcoverings when installing a new partition wall. In addition, you'll need a strategy for dealing with the ceiling junction. A plain, painted ceiling is pretty easy, but it's a bit more complicated if you have an acoustical tile or drop-down ceiling. Whether or not you remove any ceiling materials, you will need access to the ceiling joists (and floor joists) to secure the partition wall.

In just about every case, it makes sense to use 2 × 4 construction to build the partition wall frame. Even if your house is built with 24-inches on-center stud spacing, use 16 inch on-center for the partition wall. If soundproofing is a concern, you can fill the wall cavities with fiberglass batt insulation. It is unlikely that you will need to include a vapor barrier on either side of the new wall.

Choose the precise location for the new wall carefully—if at all possible, locate it so that you can tie it into existing studs and joists without having to add blocking (see page 129). Plan new stud placement before you begin. Be sure to include a pair of studs (the full-height king studs and the door rough opening-height jack stud) on each side of the door opening. Carefully read the instructions that come with your prehung interior door before building the partition wall frame as the rough opening requirements can vary. Standard widths are 30, 32, and 36 inches; standard height is 80 inches.

The basement partition wall being framed here has a rough opening for a bifold door instead of a typical passage door.

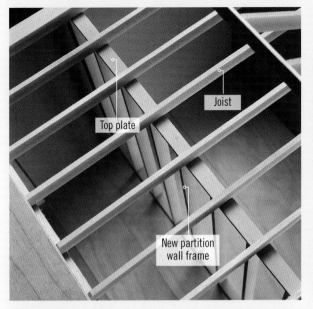

Perpendicular to joists. The easiest way to anchor a partition wall, at both the top and the bottom, is to run it perpendicular to the existing ceiling and/or floor joists. In this case, you can attach the cap plate and the sole plate directly to each joist they cross, even if you choose not to remove the ceiling or floor covering.

Parallel to joists. The most logical and practical location for your new partition wall may be parallel to the ceiling and/or floor joists. If so, you may be able to locate the wall so it is directly below a joist to which you can secure the cap plate. For a sturdier connection and a bit more flexibility on locale, add 2 × 4 blocking in the cavity between the joists and then attach the wall plate to the blocking. This, unfortunately, involves removing the ceiling to expose the cavity so you can fit and attach the blocking, but it's a very secure way to connect the new wall.

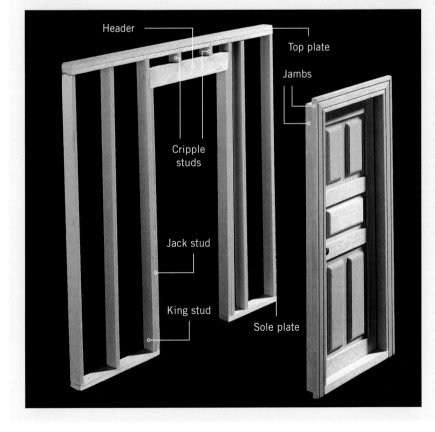

Parts of a partition wall. Non-loadbearing partition walls are relatively simple. They include a 2 × 4 top plate (sometimes doubled) attached to the ceiling joists; a bottom plate attached to the floor joists; wall studs attached to the existing, adjoining walls studs; and door framing that has a study header, cripple studs on top, and king studs and jack studs to create the door rough opening.

How to Frame a Partition Wall

TOOLS AND MATERIALS

Stud finder	Sole plate	Reciprocating saw
Pencil	3-inch construction	Eye protection
Chalkline	screws	Ear protection
Saw	2 × 4 studs	Gloves
Square	16d nails	
Cap plate	10d nails	

1. Shut off electrical power at the main service panel.

2. Determine the exact location of the partition wall separating your rooms.

3. Use a stud finder to locate and mark all framing members within the project area.

4. Mark the ends of the wall on the ceiling and floor, then snap chalklines between the points to create straight reference lines perpendicular to the existing walls.

5. Cut the cap (top) plate and sole (bottom) plate to length and lay them side by side on a flat surface with the ends flush.

6. Gang-mark the stud locations for all framing members onto both plates, using a square as a guide (Photo A).

7. Drive construction screw through the top plate and into the ceiling joists to attach the cap plate. Make sure to orient the top plate correctly and align it with your reference chalklines (Photo B).

8. Cut the studs to length and drive 16d nails through the underside of the base plate and into the ends of the studs. *Tip:* Cut each stud about ⅛ inches overlong so it fits snugly in place without falling out of alignment. Use at least two nails per stud (Photo C).

9. Raise the complete assembly in position exactly beneath the top plate and nail the base plate to the floor joists. *Note:* It's best to install the plate intact and then cut out the section of plate in the door opening later.

Use a square to gang-mark locations for all studs onto the top and sole plates.

Follow your reference lines to position the plate against the ceiling and attach it at joist locations with construction screws.

Driving 16d nails through the base plate and into the stud ends is easier and more secure then toenailing the studs after installing the base plate.

10. Fasten the end studs to the existing wall studs or blocking with 16d nails or long [116] construction screws. Make sure the end studs align exactly with the base and cap plates (Photo D). Adjust the tops of the studs as necessary until they are precisely in position, and then attach them to the top plate by toe-nailing or toe-screwing through the studs and into the plate. Be sure to get at least one fastener on each side of the wall stud (Photo E).

11. Face-nail the jack stud to the king stud on each side of the door opening with 10d nails (Photo F). Refer to your door packaging for the recommended size of the rough opening. Generally, it is ½ inch larger than the dimensions of a prehung door, including the jambs.

Position the loose ends of the studs against the top plate following the reference lines and then toenail the studs to the plate.

Fasten the end studs to the adjoining walls with nails or screws at the existing stud or blocking locations.

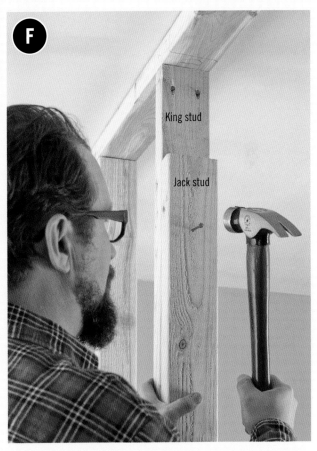

King stud

Jack stud

Face-nail the jack studs to the king studs to create a properly dimensioned rough opening for your door.

12. Rest the door header (see below) on the tops of the jack studs so it is flush with both sides of the wall framing. Nail through the king studs and into the ends of the header.

13. Cut the cripple studs to serve as a nailing surface for your wallcoverings.

- For a standard 32- to 36 inch-wide door opening, cut a cripple stud to fit the distance from the top of the header to the cap plate and center it into the opening.

- For door openings wider than 36 inches, cut as many cripple studs as you need to maintain 16-inch on-center spacing.

14. Toenail screws through the outer edges of the cripple stud into the cap plate and header (Photo G).

DOOR HEADER

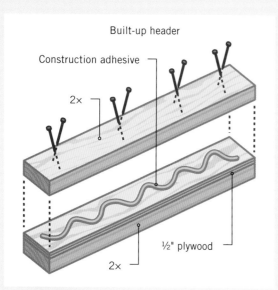

Built-up header

Construction adhesive

2×

½" plywood

2×

The top of the door rough opening is the header. Since partition walls such as this are non-loadbearing it is permissible to simply cut a 2 × 4 to the width of the rough opening and install it flat on the tops of the jack studs. It is better to construct a header consisting of two lengths of 2× stock (2 × 4 is usually adequate) sandwiching a 3½-inch-wide strip of ½-inch-thick plywood. Use screws and construction adhesive to bind the three-part, built-up header together.

15. At the bottom of the door opening, cut the base plate for the wall so it is flush with the king studs at each side of the opening. The easiest way to do this is with a blade installed upside-down in a reciprocating saw (Photo H). You'll probably need a hand saw to finish each cut. Remove the cut section of base plate.

After you secure the header, cut and install a cripple stud centered in the opening and between the header and the cap plate.

Cut and remove the section of base plate within the door rough opening.

How to Wire a Partition Wall

N ow is the time to install electrical cables, receptacles, and other devices. Most building codes require a minimum number of electrical outlets, usually six feet apart, in any permanent wall. You'll almost surely want them anyway, especially if you are creating a home office. Plus, the new room should have a light switch close to the door opening that operates a light—not necessarily a ceiling fixture—that illuminates the entire room. If you are experienced and comfortable working with wiring, you can install it yourself. Otherwise, hire a professional electrician. Either way, you will need a permit and an inspection before you cover the work. Do not make the hookups until your work is inspected and approved.

INSULATION?

Adding a new partition wall in an existing room probably does not require that you include wall insulation for heating and cooling improvements, and most cases won't require a moisture (vapor) barrier. However, if you will use the new room as an office or even a bedroom, consider adding insulation in the stud cavities for sound control.

While there are insulation products, often employing mineral wool, designed specifically to enhance sound abatement, standard, unfaced fiberglass batts are cheap, easy, and will make a significant improvement. Wear the appropriate protective gear to pack the batts (don't overpack) into the cavities after the wiring is in place and one side of the partition wall has a wallcovering.

Tip: If there are cables in the wall cavity, split the batt into two half-thick pieces. Install one half behind the cables and the other half in front of them. See page 20 for more information on soundproofing.

Contractors may differ on when it's ideal to install electrical cables and boxes, but certainly the best access to a framed partition wall is before you cover the walls.

How to Install Wall Coverings on a Partition Wall

You probably want to cover your new partition with drywall. "Rocking" and then taping and mudding drywall is no one's favorite job, but it is economical, durable, and paintable compared to other, less common options, such as paneling. If light weight and ease of installation of paneling is attractive to you, though, go for it.

The standard for interior walls is ½-inch-thick panels that are sold in 4 × 8-foot sheets. Be aware that, except for special ultralight panels, a typical sheet of ½-inch drywall weighs nearly 60 pounds. You'll appreciate having a helper to lift and adjust panels, and you'll get better results.

Even professional drywallers disagree over whether it is better to install the panels vertically or horizontally. In general, horizontal panel installation is slightly more efficient for larger, flat walls, if only because it creates long, horizontal seams that are easier to tape and finish. For a smallish partition wall in an existing room, the advantage is negligible. *Note:* If you are building in a high-moisture area, such as a basement, look for moisture and mold-resistant panels. Some codes may require this.

TOOLS AND MATERIALS
1 ¼-inch Type W drywall screws

Drill

Construction adhesive

Foot-operated panel-lifter (optional)

Drywall saw

Drywall tape

Tape knife

Lightweight drywall compound

Sandpaper

Respiratory protection

Eye protection

Gloves

A foot-operated panel lifter helps maintain an even ½-inch gap between each panel and the floor.

Three thin layers of compound tapered with increasingly broad taping knives is how the pros do it. Sand and paint.

1. Run a bead of construction adhesive along each stud and screw the drywall panels in place. Recess the screwheads slightly to avoid rupturing the paper covering.

Tip: A standard cordless drill/driver will work fine, especially if you set the clutch low so the drill stops as soon as the screwhead is just countersunk. You can also buy or rent dedicated drywall screw guns, some of which can be fitted with auto-feeding screw coils.

2. Cut around door and electrical box locations.

3. Tape the seams, cover the screwheads, and install folded tape or corner bead at the wall and ceiling junctions.

4. Apply and sand drywall compound, making sure to wear appropriate respiratory protection.

If you don't have much drywall experience, investigate the many good books and other information sources, including manufacturer websites, that describe drywall installation in more detail.

Doors

A partition wall without a door is close to useless. Choosing the right door is basically a matter of ease, cost, and design. Do also consider light, privacy, and, in some cases, security.

Installing a prehung interior door in your new partition wall is a relatively easy job.

You can add swinging French doors to an open passageway between two rooms to divide the space while providing full visibility and sound privacy without creating a sense of isolation.

A full light glass door mounted on a door tracking system is a contemporary style with the same benefits as a traditional multi-lite French door. Here, the extended door tracks include sliding solid wood doors that conceal the storage area.

Door Types

Prehung passage doors. Most homeowners choose basic hollow-core prehung interior doors. They are economical, easy to install, and most are predrilled with holes for the handleset and strikeplate. They come in enough styles, from solid slabs to various raised panel configurations, that matching your existing doors' style—or at least coming close—should not be difficult. Be aware though that many of the nonstandard designs will be special order, so you'll want to allow at least two to four weeks for delivery.

French doors. There are other options to a solid, swinging door. French doors, for example, allow light and sight into and out of the new room. Though not be ideal for a bedroom, it can make the separate area more comfortable and less isolated. Typical French doors consist of two doors with multi-light panels from top to bottom. The doors swing open on the outside and close together. The muntins and mullions (the cross-hatch of retainer panels) add classic design appeal. You can hang them in a door opening in a new partition wall or even create a frame around a small room, alcove, or foyer to block out space for a small office.

Barn door hardware. A rise in the popularity of the Farmhouse style has led to a boom in the options available for sliding barn doors. For those with more wall space than open space, this door style is an efficient option. A rod or track attached at ceiling stud locations above and past the door opening supports the sliding hangers that attach to the top of the doors, allowing them to slide completely to the side, like a pocket door mounted on the wall's exterior. Door guides mounted to the floor prevent outswing as the door moves. Typical barn doors are solid and rustic, but you can use the hardware to hang sliding French doors, retaining the advantages of the multi-lite panels but eliminating the swing radius required by a hinged door.

Preserve the open, light feel of French doors without sacrificing swing space by mounting one or more multi-lite panels on sliding barn door hardware.

How to Hang a Prehung Interior Door

Prehung door technology has made the once-tricky process of hanging a door almost foolproof. As the name implies, the door comes from the manufacturer preinstalled with hinges in the door jamb frame. As long as you manage to secure the jambs squarely into the door opening, it should work just fine out of the box.

After removing the door, make sure it swings within the opening. Manufacturers often secure the doors for transport with a nail or two driven through the jambs or with strapping material. Make sure the opening is clear and carefully set the door and jamb frame assembly in the opening. The edges of the jambs should be flush with the wall surfaces surrounding the door opening. The required space beneath the door should be preset by the side jambs as they rest on the floor.

For ease of installation and economy, a wooden prehung passage door is hard to beat. It offers full privacy, lockability, and can introduce some warm wood tones to a room or be painted.

TOOLS AND MATERIALS

Prehung interior door
Level
Wood shims
Hammer
8d casing nails
Handsaw
Case molding
Drill
4d finish nails

1. Set the prehung door in the opening with the jambs flush to the wall surfaces. Use a level to make sure the door is plumb in the opening, concentrating primarily on the hinge side (Photo A).

2. Insert pairs of wood shims into the gap between the hinge-side jamb and the wall stud in the rough opening. You'll likely have to hold the shims together for the first pair or two, as they tend to want to clatter out. The goal is to get even gaps all around the door frame.

Add shims to square the door in the opening, checking for plumb as you go.

OPTION: BARN DOOR HARDWARE

Sliding barn door hardware has become more readily available in recent years as Farmhouse home styles have grown in popularity. In addition to allowing you to use beautiful oversize door panels, the mechanism is highly space efficient as long as you have open wall space equal in width to the door opening. A rod or track is attached at stud locations above the door opening and supports the sliding hangers that are attached to the top of the door so it can move easily side to side. Door guides are mounted on the floor to prevent outswing as the door moves.

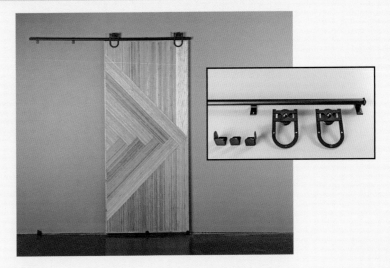

Secure the door jambs to the framing members in the rough opening, starting with the hinge side. Use 8d casing nails driven through shim pairs at 12-in. intervals.

After shimming and nailing both sides and the head jamb, trim off the ends of the shims with a handsaw.

Locknail the mitered joints in the door casing at the tops by driving a 4d nail through both joints. Predrilling is a good idea.

3. Drive 8d casing nails through the jamb and shim pairs and into the jack stud at the edge of the door rough opening (Photo B). Drive a nail every 12 inches or so, testing the jamb for plumb as you work and adjusting as necessary.

4. Once the hinge-side jamb is secure and plumb, add shim pairs and 8d nails above the head jamb and the header and between the latch-side jamb and the wall stud. Test the swing of the door.

5. Trim off the ends of all shims so they do not project past the wall surfaces (Photo C).

6. Install case molding around the door opening on both sides. Case molding is sold premitered in three-stick sets. Install the head piece first and then the side casing, maintaining a slight but consistent reveal all the way around the frame. To prevent the mitered joints from opening up, drill pilot holes and then locknail the joints with 4d finish nails driven through each joint (Photo D).

How to Install a Door Handleset

Most readily available prehung doors come pre-drilled for the handleset, which includes the handles and the latch bolt that fits into the strike plate on the latch-side jamb. Make sure that you buy the right size for your door, and this depends on door thickness. The other critical distance is the backset: the distance from the edge of the door to the centerpoint of the main handleset hole. Today, this is almost assuredly going to be either 2⅜ inches or 2¾ inches. Most handleset mechanisms can be adjusted to fit either (Photo A).

Insert the cylindrical latch bolt into the 1 inch-diameter hole in the door edge. Use a hammer and a piece of scrap wood to rap onto the bolt and set it into the wood on the side of the cutout (Photo B). Note: If your door has a rectangular mortise around the latch

bolt hole, look in the handleset kit for a mounting plate that fits into the mortise. If your door simply has the round hole, you do not need the plate.

One half of the handleset will have a flat spindle attached. Insert the spindle into the slotted hole in the latch bolt (Photo C). From the other side of the door, slip the other half of the handleset into the opening and try to align the long mounting screws with their corresponding screwholes in the latch bolt (Photo D). This can be a little fussy. Once you have registered the mounting screws, tighten them to draw the two halves of the handleset tightly together. Test the operation. Finally, screw the latch bolt strike plate into the jamb mortise, making sure to orient it to work with the door swing direction (Photo E).

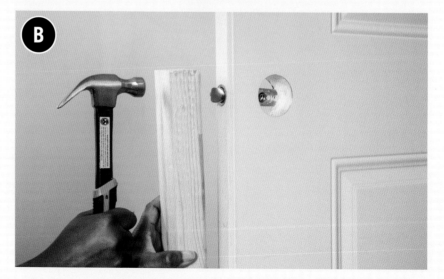

Adjust the latch bolt settings to match your setback distance: 2⅛ in. or 2¾ in.

Insert the latch bolt into the pre-drilled 1 in.-diameter hole and rap it to set the end of the bolt into the inside edge of the handleset hole.

Insert the flat spindle through one half of the handleset cylinder and into the mating slot in the latch bolt.

Align the long mounting screws in the other half of the handleset with the mating holes in the latch bolt and tighten.

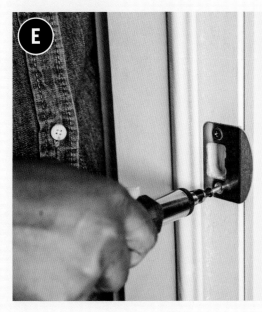

Install the latch strike plate in the pre-drilled mortise in the door jamb.

Bookcase Room Dividers

It makes perfect sense that most people build bookcases and shelving flat against room walls. But, building them perpendicular to the room walls defines space while providing storage that is often accessible from both sides of the unit. Set some nice plants or artwork on top and even an eye-level bookcase becomes a substantial room divider.

If you live in an apartment or condo, or just appreciate the option to adjust your space, a freestanding bookcase is probably a better choice than a built-in one. You can buy them just about anywhere, often in flat packs that are relatively easy to assemble. But be aware that most freestanding bookcases rely on the stability of the wall behind them—some even have safety straps that are intended to be attached to the wall to prevent the bookcase from toppling.

Projecting the bookcase or shelving unit out into the room makes it more vulnerable, so look for ways to either anchor the freestanding unit or opt for adding a built-in unit and securing it to the adjoining wall and floor—and to the ceiling if it's a floor-to-ceiling design. A built-in unit is less mobile, of course, but much more stable, and it allows you to carry over trim and other elements of the existing room design.

Whether partial- or full-height, freestanding or built-in, a bookcase or open shelving structure is a great tool for compartmentalizing space while also providing much-needed storage.

Built-In Room-Divider Bookcase

The foyer or entryway often represents some of the least-utilized space in your home. It also is where the first impression is made on guests. Shrinking the space with a well-designed built-in bookcase creates an enhanced sense of intimacy upon entry while affording the chance to add utility with an attached entry bench and coat hooks, as in this project. If the goal is to define a workspace or a visiting/receiving area, this project does that, too. You can welcome visitors, business-related or otherwise, without the inconvenience of having guests traipse through your house to reach a remote home office.

TOOLS AND MATERIALS

Table saw	2" wood screws
Miter saw	1" wood screws
Drill/driver	1¼" fine thread pocket screws
Router	(6) No. 8 × 1¼" panhead
45 degree bottom-bearing chamfer bit	screws
	(6) Washers
Air compressor	Wood glue
Brad nail gun	(2) 2"-long × 1½"-wide butt
(2) 1 × 2 × 8-ft. solid oak	hinges
(3) 1 × 4 × 8-ft. solid oak	¼"-dia. shelf pins
1 × 6 × 8-ft. solid oak	(1) Left mount lid support–
(2) ¾ × 4 × 8 oak veneered plywood	Rockler No. 26195
	(4) Coat hooks
(1) ¼ × 4 × 8 oak veneered plywood	Eye and ear protection
	Work gloves

A useful, matching entry bench stabilizes this built-in bookcase/room divider at the home's entryway. Both are attached and also fastened to the wall and floor for permanence and stability.

ROOM DIVIDER BOOKCASE

BACK VIEW

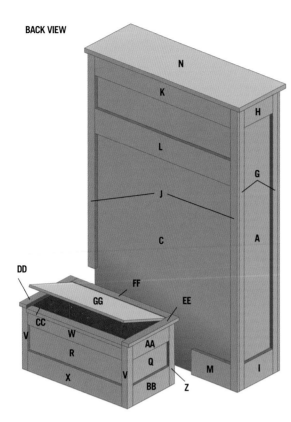

FRONT VIEW

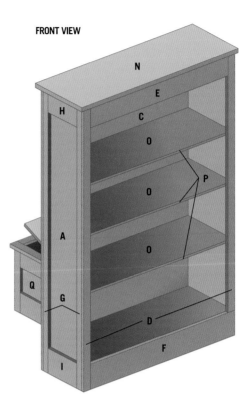

KEY	NO.	DESCRIPTION	DIMENSION	KEY	NO.	DESCRIPTION	DIMENSION
A	2	Bookcase sides	¾ × 11 × 66"	R	1	Bench front	¾ × 15¼ × 35¼"
B	2	Bookcase top and bottom	¾ × 11 × 46½"	S	1	Bench back	¾ × 16 × 35¼"
C	1	Bookcase back	¾ × 48 × 66"	T	1	Bench bottom, plywood	¾ × 14½ × 35¼"
D	2	Bookcase front frame stiles	¾ × 2¼ × 66"	U	1	Bench lid rail	¾ × 2¼ × 35¼"
E	1	Bookcase front frame top rail	¾ × 3½ × 44½"	V	2	Bench front frame stiles	¾ × 2¼ × 16"
F	1	Bookcase front frame bottom rail	¾ × 5½ × 44½"	W	1	Bench front frame top rail	¾ × 3½ × 33¼"
G	2	Bookcase side frame stiles	¾ × 1½ × 66"	X	1	Bench front frame bottom rail	¾ × 5½ × 33¼"
H	1	Bookcase side frame top rail	¾ × 3½ × 8¼"	Y	1	Bench side frame left stile	¾ × 1½ × 16"
I	1	Bookcase side frame bottom rail	¾ × 5½ × 8¼"	Z	1	Bench side frame right stile	¾ × 2¼ × 16"
J	2	Bookcase back frame stiles	¾ × 2¼ × 66"	AA	1	Bench side frame top rail	¾ × 3½ × 12¼"
K	1	Bookcase back top rail	¾ × 3½ × 44½"	BB	1	Bench side frame bottom rail	¾ × 5½ × 12¼"
L	1	Bookcase back middle rail	¾ × 5½ × 44½"	CC	1	Bench front cap	¾ × 1½ × 35¼"
M	1	Bookcase back bottom rail	¾ × 5½ × 9"	DD	1	Bench left cap	¾ × 2¼ × 17"
N	1	Finished top	¾ × 13¼ × 49¼"	EE	1	Bench right side cap	¾ × 2½ × 17"
O	3	Shelves	¾ × 10¾ × 46¼"	FF	1	Bench back cap	¾ × 2¼ × 33¼"
P	3	Shelf edge	¾ × 1 × 46¼"	GG	1	Bench lid	¾ × 14½ × 33"
Q	2	Bench sides	¾ × 16 × 16"	HH	2	Lid support cleats	¾ × 2¼ × 3"

How to Build a Room-Divider Bookcase

This project uses hardwood veneer plywood (oak as shown) and a few pieces of hardwood dimensional lumber. For a lighter appearance, you can choose species such as maple, birch, or poplar. Most building centers sell them in both plywood and 8-foot dimensional lumber.

1. Cut the side, bottom, and top panels to size from ¾-inch plywood. When joined together into a box shape, these parts comprise what is called the carcase.

2. Drill the ¼-inch shelf pin holes, making sure they align side to side. It's easier to access the side panels for drilling before assembling the carcase.

3. **Tip:** A piece of ¼-inch perforated hardboard makes a handy guide for spacing the holes. Wrap a piece of masking tape on the drill bit as a depth guide. The holes should be ⅜-inch deep. For maximum flexibility with shelf height, drill a hole every inch, which should correspond to the hole spacing on the perf board. Locate the holes 1 inch from the edges of the side panels (Photo A).

4. Apply wood glue to each joint and clamp the panels together. Make sure the carcase is square and all of the edges are flush.

5. Drill pilot holes in the side panels and into the top and bottom panel, then drive 2-inch wood screws through pilot holes (Photo B).

6. Cut the back panel for the bookcase to size from ¼ inch-thick hardwood plywood. Its edges should be flush with the outer edges of the carcase.

7. Drive 1-inch brads through the back panel and into the back edges of the plywood carcase.

8. Apply wood glue to the edges of the front and back panels of the

Use perforated hardboard as a guide to drilling the shelf-pin holes.

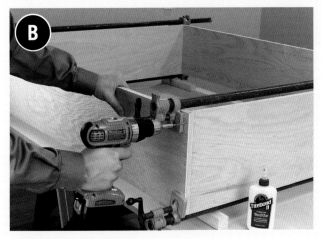

Assemble the carcase with glue and screws.

TOOLS

One key to the success of this project is to get straight cuts on the plywood case parts. A table saw or panel-cutting saw practically guarantees perfectly straight cuts. You can still achieve straight and square workpieces with a circular saw and a straightedge cutting guide.

Most saw blade manufacturers sell blades designed specifically for plywood. A 7 ¼-inch blade with 40 teeth (compared to a general 24-tooth blade) will yield clean, splinter-free cuts here. To make this project as shown, you'll also need a router or laminate trimmer with a chamfer bit to shape the decorative profiles on the face frames, although you could make the cuts with a hand plane or even a sander, if you are careful.

A pocket-screw jig made it easy to drive pocket screws for the face frame joints. You have other joinery options, such as dowel joints or biscuit joints, if you do not want to use pocket screws.

Attach the lid rail between the carcase sides.

Use a pocket-hole jig as a guide to drill the pocket screw guide holes.

Assemble the face frames with glue and pocket screws.

Make chamfer cuts on the face frame with a router.

FACE FRAMES

Hardwood face frames fitted to the sides and front of both the bookcase and the bench conceal the plywood edges and stiffen the carcases. If you wish to use pocket hole screws to join the frames, as seen here, square-cut all of the face frame parts to the dimensions in the cutting list—a power miter saw is perfect for this job. Use a pocket hole jig and a drill/driver fitted with a stepped pocket-hole bit to drill the pocket screw guide holes in the mating parts (Photo D). Create each face frame by fastening the mating parts together with glue and 1 ¼-inch fine-thread pocket screws (Photo E).

Each face frame features decorative profile cuts on the outer edges of the frame parts, inside each frame opening. The best tool to cut these is a router fitted with a piloted, 45° chamfer bit. Use stop blocks in the frame corners to keep from cutting the profiles too close to the corner. Cut all the chamfers. You'll get better results if you make each cut in two passes of increasing depth (Photo F.) Note: Since these are purely decorative cuts you can skip them if you wish, or simply break the edges of the frame parts with a sander.

Starting on the sides, use a pneumatic brad nailer and glue to attach the face frame to the carcases. Or, use glue and 4d finish nails driven into pilot holes. Then, attach the front and back face frames to the sides (Photo G).

bench, attach the side panels, check for square, and clamp.

9. Drill countersunk pilot holes and drive the screws into them, checking for square as you work.

10. Cut the bench lid rail and screw it into place between the side panels, flush with their tops and 1 inch in from the back panel (Photo C).

11. Cut the pieces for the cap that frames the bench opening. Include a ¾ × ¾-inch notch at each end of the front cap piece so it fits around the stiles of the front frame pieces (Photo H).

12. Install the cap with glue and nails or brads.

13. Cut the shelves for the bookcase to size.

14. Attach 1 × 2 edging flush with each shelf board top and ends to conceal the plywood edge grain. Use glue and brads or nails.

15. Cut strips of dimensional lumber 1 to 2 inches longer than the final dimension of the bench lid and

Attach the front and back face frames to the cabinet.

Attach the bench caps to the top of the bench assembly.

Edge-glue the lid from pieces of solid lumber.

Install the lid hinges and support hardware.

bookcase top and lay them out on a flat surface. The combined width should also be an inch or so longer than the final dimension. You could use plywood, but dimensional lumber will have better results.

16. Apply glue to the mating edges and clamp them together, and sandwich the glue-up boards by clamping them between wood strips (called "cauls") above and below (Photo I). A biscuit (plate) joiner will help with the alignment. Let the glue dry.

17. Unclamp the edges and the glue-ups and cut them to final size. Sand and apply finish to all wood parts.

18. Attach the bench lid to the bench back cap with the butt hinges.

19. Cut a pair of lid support cleats and install them inside the benchtop opening, at the sides and near the back.

20. Screw the lid support hardware to the lid support cleats and the lid bottom (Photo J).

21. Drill pilot holes into the carcase top. Make them slightly larger than the screw diameter to allow for wood movement.

22. Drive 1 ¼-inch panhead screws and washers through the bookcase carcase top to attach the finished top.

This room-divider bookcase is designed as a built-in, or at least to fit flush against the wall. Cut out any base trim in the installation area to nestle the unit flush against the wall. Slide the bookcase and bench into rough position, predrill pilot holes, and then attach the two with 2-inch screws driven through the bookcase and into the bench to aid stability. Slide the bookcase and bench flush against the wall, predrill pilot holes, and countersink a couple of 3-inch screws through the bookcase side and into the wall at stud locations. If there are no studs available in the installation area, insert wall anchors into the drywall at the drilled locations and then drive the anchor screws. Install the coat hooks on the bookcase back rail. Insert dowel pins into the guide holes in the bookcase at your desired shelf locations, then rest the shelves on the pins.

Desks, Shelving, and Storage

Foldaway Wall Bench/Desk

A drop-down, fold-up worksurface provides a useful center for doing homework or creating crafts, and it can virtually disappear when not in use, leaving your living space essentially uninterrupted. This sturdy version will support the biggest textbooks and also any crafting exercise, from stamping to woodcarving.

The painted, double layer of birch plywood is an easy-to-clean, highly durable and very smooth worksurface. The sturdy hinged supports keep the worksurface stable. Building this drop-down desk requires only basic woodworking skills and tools, and the materials are inexpensive. Photos by Larry Okrend.

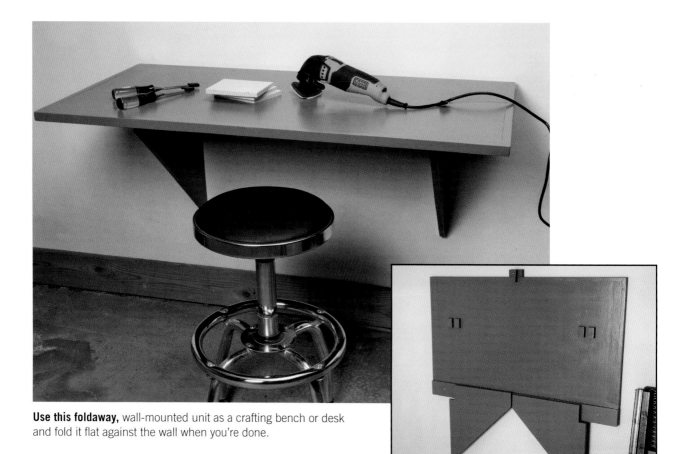

Use this foldaway, wall-mounted unit as a crafting bench or desk and fold it flat against the wall when you're done.

FOLDAWAY WALL BENCH/DESK

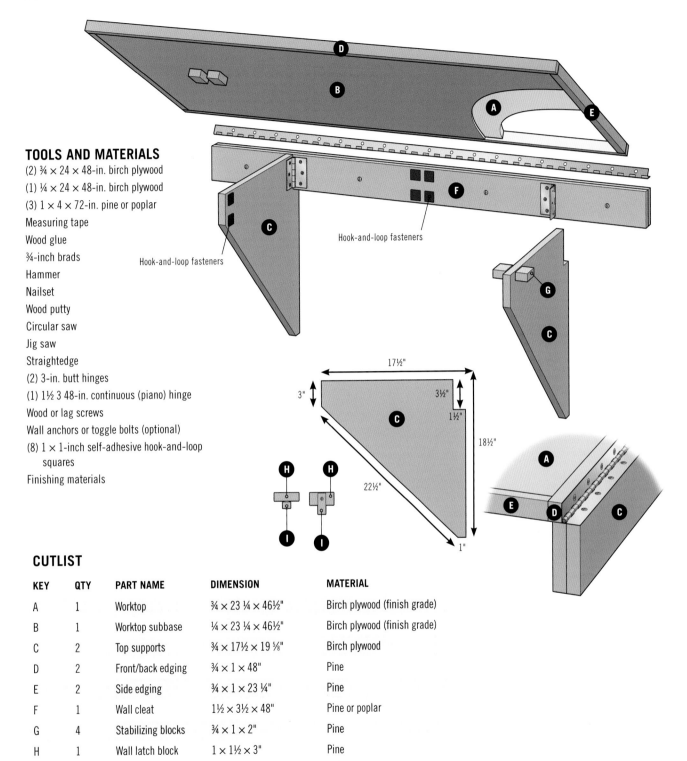

TOOLS AND MATERIALS

(2) ¾ × 24 × 48-in. birch plywood

(1) ¼ × 24 × 48-in. birch plywood

(3) 1 × 4 × 72-in. pine or poplar

Measuring tape

Wood glue

¾-inch brads

Hammer

Nailset

Wood putty

Circular saw

Jig saw

Straightedge

(2) 3-in. butt hinges

(1) 1½ 3 48-in. continuous (piano) hinge

Wood or lag screws

Wall anchors or toggle bolts (optional)

(8) 1 × 1-inch self-adhesive hook-and-loop squares

Finishing materials

Hook-and-loop fasteners

Hook-and-loop fasteners

CUTLIST

KEY	QTY	PART NAME	DIMENSION	MATERIAL
A	1	Worktop	¾ × 23 ¼ × 46½"	Birch plywood (finish grade)
B	1	Worktop subbase	¼ × 23 ¼ × 46½"	Birch plywood (finish grade)
C	2	Top supports	¾ × 17½ × 19 ⅝"	Birch plywood
D	2	Front/back edging	¾ × 1 × 48"	Pine
E	2	Side edging	¾ × 1 × 23 ¼"	Pine
F	1	Wall cleat	1½ × 3½ × 48"	Pine or poplar
G	4	Stabilizing blocks	¾ × 1 × 2"	Pine
H	1	Wall latch block	1 × 1½ × 3"	Pine
I	1	Wall latch toggle	¾ 3 1 3 2½"	Pine

Note: The birch panels shown here are cut down slightly smaller than the 2 × 4-foot "handy panels" sold at the store. Face-gluing (laminating) the worktop to the subbase creates a sturdy 1-inch-thick desktop that accepts paint or stain well. To get uniformly sized mating parts, you can laminate the top and bottom together and then trim them to size after the glue-up.

How to Build a Foldaway Wall Bench/Desk

WORKTOP

1. Apply wood glue to the mating surface of the worktop and subbase, using a glue roller and wood glue. Press the two pieces together with the edges flush. Driving ¾-inch brads up through the bottom layer for extra holding power isn't a bad idea.

2. Attach 1-inch-wide edging strips to each piece, butting the joints together with the front and back edges overlapping the sides. Keep the tops flush with the top of the worktop.

3. Set the heads of the 1½-inch finish nails with a nailset, and fill the holes with wood putty.

SUPPORTS

You can cut the two triangular top supports from a single piece of ¾-inch-thick plywood (Photo A).

1. Plot out the parts using the pattern on page 153 and then make the straight cuts with a circular saw and a straightedge. Cut the 1½ × 3½-inch notches with a jig saw (Photo B).

2. Face-glue two 1 × 4s (if you are using poplar, as here) to make the supports or cut them from a clear, straight pine 2 × 4.

3. Using the wall support as a spacer, attach the butt hinges to the top supports. When you attach the hinges to the wall support in step 5, do so at the notched top so the top supports fit flush against the wall.

4. Set the parts in position on the underside of the worktop with the stabilizing blocks set in place to help ensure that the top supports are perpendicular to the wall supports.

5. Verify that everything is squared and aligned, then finish attaching the butt hinges at all parts (Photo C).

6. Attach the worktop to the wall support with a continuous, or piano, hinge. Leave enough clearance between the parts for the knuckle of the hinge and the two parts to operate freely. Now would be a good time to sand and paint all of the parts, including the blocks and latch discussed below.

Fasten the edging strips, set the finish nails, and fill in the holes with wood putty

Plot the parts, then use a jig saw and a circular saw with a straightedge to cut out the pieces.

Top support

Butt hinge

Wall support

Stabilizing block

Make sure to square and align everything before attaching the butt hinges to all parts.

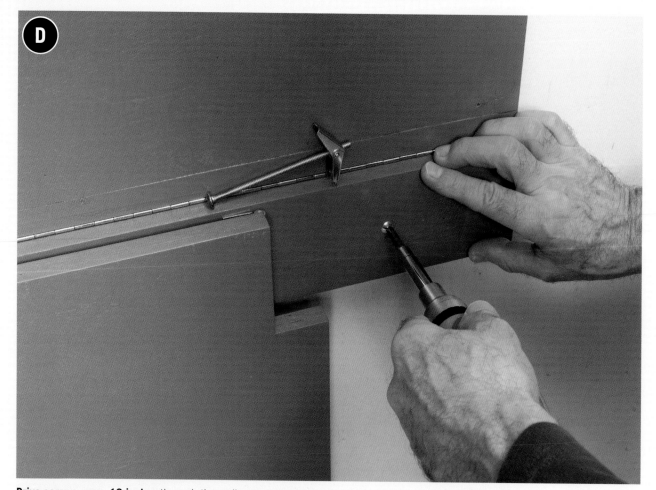

Drive screws every 12 inches through the wall support and into wall studs (best) or hollow wall anchors.

WALL-MOUNTING

Prop or tack the assembled desk/workbench unit in position against the wall. The working height of the surface should be 32 to 36 inches above the floor—choose a working height that is comfortable for you or the user. Attach the unit to the wall with wood screws or lag screws. Try to locate the screws so they will hit wall studs when driven through the wall support. Where no studs are available, use hollow wall anchors (or toggle bolts) to accept the screws. Drive a screw with minimum spacing of 12 inches (Photo D).

STABILIZING BLOCKS AND WALL LATCH

Attached to the underside of the worktop, the stabilizing blocks sandwich the top supports when you lower the top onto the them and prevent lateral movement. Drill pilot holes and then attach the blocks with glue and finish nails.

The two-part wall latch assembly includes a block and a toggle. The former attaches to the wall just above the top of the worktop when it's folded against the wall. The toggle attaches to the block with a screw that isn't fully driven so you can spin the toggle. With the top pressed flat against the wall, spin the toggle downward to trap the top securely.

Add self-adhesive 1 × 1-inch hook-and-loop tabs to the wall supports and to the inside faces of the top supports. These secure the supports when the top is in the raised position (Photo E).

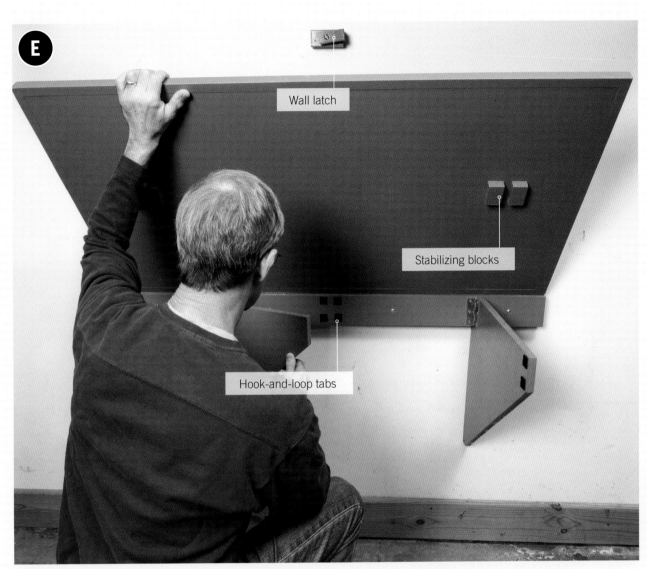

E

Wall latch

Stabilizing blocks

Hook-and-loop tabs

The wall latch, stabilizing blocks, and hook-and-loop tabs keep the worktop secure whether it is lowered or raised.

Understairs Solutions

With some imagination and a little work, you can transform the understairs area in your house from a dark, forgotten alcove into a bustling focal point. You can fit shelving, drawers, and cabinets into the wedge-shaped area, or, with a few modifications, convert the space into a functional home office. Pull-out shelves repurpose an understairs area near a kitchen as a convenient pantry. A staircase near your front or back door can house a coat rack and boot benches. And what better place to build a convenient wine cellar than to tuck it beneath a staircase? Reading nooks, coat closets, powder rooms, laundry centers—the list is practically endless.

Drawers neatly fill the lower end of this understairs area and terminate at desk height to support a desktop while leaving knee space at the high end.

This project does a fine job of combining two great hardworking home strategies: understairs solutions plus a closet office (see page 80).

Modifying utility stairs, for example anchoring a simple shelf system to the basement case under-carriage, can up the value of little-used space.

An L-shaped work center knits in seamlessly to the underside of this open-side staircase. Storage cubicles reflect the steps up to desk height and even beyond.

This home office makes the most of a very small area. The built-in shelving leaves just enough room for a computer table and a narrow file cabinet.

Mounting track lights on the stair stringer transforms this dreary corner into a brightly defined office space with no further remodeling required.

Finishing an Understairs Area

In most homes, the area beneath a staircase is enclosed. If not, it probably is finished with wallcoverings to match the rest of the room, possibly functioning as a passthrough space between rooms. Open staircases in modern homes create usable space that holds little remodeling potential. If your staircase is closed off and there is nothing occupying the space beneath it, you can reclaim the area with a project such as this fairly fancy bookcase.

If you are averse to working with weird angles, creating storage or office space underneath a staircase can be frustrating. There are workarounds, especially if the understairs area is unfinished, as in a basement. But if your staircase fronts a living area where you are seeking to maintain some design standards, think carefully before you cut into any walls to expose the space.

Having said that, transforming an understairs area into a functional space or even a living/working space is a very rewarding way to make your house into a more hardworking home. This project is an example of the challenges you will encounter and how you can meet them. Proceed when you are confident you will be taking it on.

This high-style birch bookcase project is just one example of how you can transform the wasted area beneath the steps into a highly useful and even attractive space.

How to Build an Understairs Bookcase

TOOLS AND MATERIALS

Pencil
2 × 4s
Nails
Measuring tape
Cabinet-grade plywood (birch shown here)
Wood glue
Wood screws
Miter saw or miter box
Saw
1-inch screws
1 × 2 edging

This project uses the strategy of building a couple of manageable cabinet frames (*carcases*) that you can slide into the opening and join together.

1. Mark the stud locations, the bottoms of the stair stringers, and any electrical service or other elements that may reside within the walled area. This will help you to visualize your project and make a plan with real measurements (Photo A). Make your plan. Studs are primarily nailing surfaces for attaching the wallcovering, but you should consult a construction engineer if you are not sure whether the studs are non-loadbearing.

2. Clean out the area thoroughly.

3. If you are installing cabinets or shelving, install "sleepers" on the floor, which are 2 × 4s nailed down at the front of the opening and placed perpendicular to the back wall and front sleeper at standard stud wall

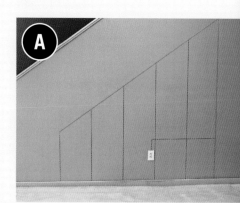

Mark the project layout area and any wall elements on the wall surface.

spacing, usually 16-inches on-center. This creates a sturdy and level base for the project.

4. Cut plywood strips (this project uses cabinet-grade birch plywood) and assemble the two trapezoidal frames with glue and wood screws at the joints (Photo B). Using screws, fasten the shelves that fit within the upright frame panels. Slide the taller unit onto the sleepers and anchor it with screws.

5. Build L-shaped shelf/divider inserts with beveled edges where they meet the sloping frames. Install them at the top of the opening (Photo C). Create the second unit the same way so it is as complete as possible when you slide it in next to the first unit. Check that the front edges of the two units are flush and aligned, and then anchor the second unit to the floor. Drive some 1-inch countersunk screws to secure the two units together.

6. Cut and attach 1 × 2 edging to conceal the exposed plywood grain. The horizontal edging strips should run uninterrupted, with the vertical strips butting against them (Photo D). Cut trim strips to conceal the area between the new understairs units and the wall surface (Photo E).

You can stop now if you wish and simply apply a finish. If you'd rather have showy cabinet doors, as opposed to open shelving, build cabinet doors that close over the shelving.

The cabinet doors in this project feature clear plexiglass panels that fit into recesses routed into the inside edges of the door face-frame openings. You can use glass, but these doors will be low to the ground and relatively vulnerable. Make the door face frames by measuring the angles and lengths and cutting rails and stiles for each door. Try to maintain a consistent line on the angle formed by the tops of the door face frames once you install them. Pocket screws are the perfect joinery method for making the face frames.

Use a router and a wood chisel to create the recesses for the clear cabinet panels, and install them with glaziers' points or tack strips. Hang the doors and install latch hardware.

Cut plywood tops, bottoms, and sides for each trapezoidal carcase unit and join the parts with glue and wood screws.

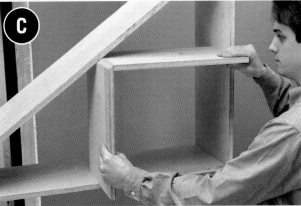

Attach the L-shaped inserts at the tops of the openings.

Attach 1 × 2 shelf edging to all exposed edges, butting the edges of the vertical strips against the horizontal ones.

Cover the gaps between the new project and the old wall surface with wood trim.

Utility Shelves

A reliable set of utility shelves can provide on-demand storage within a room to make it more functional or create storage that allows you to empty out a room inside the house and use it for something else. Built from everyday 2 × 4s and plywood and designed for a room with an 8-foot ceiling, the utility shelves in this project are very simple. The necessary tools are basic as well, depending on how you feel about routers (one was used to cut the shelf grooves).

A simple but spacious shelf system provides efficient storage so you can better use other areas of your home.

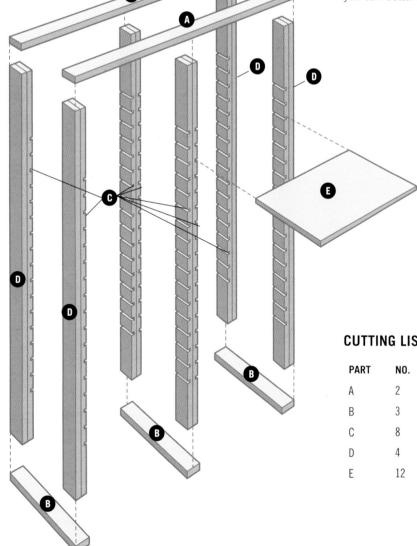

TOOLS AND MATERIALS

(15) 2 × 4 × 8
(2) ¾ in. × 4 × 8 ft. plywood
Saw
Router
¾-in. straight bit
Wood glue
Shims
Measuring tape
Powder-actuated nailer (optional, used for concrete flooring)
Drill
Screws (2½ in., 3 in.)

CUTTING LIST

PART	NO.	DESC.	SIZE	MATERIAL
A	2	Top plates	68"	2 × 4
B	3	Sole plates	24"	2 × 4
C	8	Shelf risers	93"	2 × 4
D	4	End risers	93"	2 × 4
E	12	Shelves	30¾ × 24"	plywood

How to Build Utility Shelves

Carefully align the sole plates with the top plates. Use a powder-actuated nailer to attach the sole plates to a concrete floor (inset).

Join middle shelf support standards with pairs of grooved risers. Place the risers back to back and align the grooves.

Attach the end and middle riser pairs to the top plate and sole plate with 3-inch screws.

Cut plywood shelves to fit and slide them into the opposing grooves in the standards in any configuration you choose.

Alignment is key to this shelving unit project.

1. Attach the top plates to the ceiling or rafters and parallel to the wall, with the front and back edges 24 inches apart.

2. Attach the sole plates to the floor, making sure their outside corners are directly below the outside corners of the top plates. Use 3-inch screws for a wood subbase over joists or a powder-actuated nailer if the floor is concrete (Photo A).

3. Cut the 2 × 4 shelf risers to the height of the room minus 3 inches and lay them on a flat surface with the ends aligned.

4. Clamp the risers together edge-to-edge and cut 7/8-inch-wide × ¾-inch-deep dado grooves across the faces at intervals of around 6 inches to create the shelf-supporting grooves. A router with a ¾-inch straight bit is best for this.

5. Join two pairs of grooved risers together back-to-back with glue and 2½-inch screws to create the middle shelf supports (Photo B). Pair each remaining grooved riser with an uncut 2 × 4 of the same length, and join the pairs to create the outer shelf standards.

6. Fit an outer shelf standard pair between the cap and sole plates at each end, grooves facing inward. Toenail 3-inch screws through the standards and into the plates (Photo C).

7. Cut ¾-inch plywood shelves to fit between the grooves in the standards. Size them to be flush with the outside front and back edges of the standards and ¼-inch narrower than the distance from the opposing grooves, measured from the bottoms of the grooves. Make as many shelves as you care to, and insert them into the opposing grooves (Photo D).

Pegboard, also called perforated hardboard or perfboard, can be fou[nd] any building center and most hardware stores.

Pegboard Storage

Pegboard (technically called perforated hardboard) is an inexpensive and readily available sheet good that is easy to convert into a hanging storage center. Although we tend to think of it as a wall storage system for garages and basements, you can dress it up with paint and a nice frame. Buy it in 4 × 8 panels or more manageable 4 × 4-foot or 2 × 4-foot handy panels. It comes in ⅛-inch and ¼-inch thicknesses, the latter of which are heavier and costlier but also much more durable and rigid.

You'll usually find both plain and tempered pegboard. The tempered product, which is darker brown, is coated with linseed oil and fired, which makes it more rigid, stronger, more resistant to moisture, and easier to clean—but also harder to paint. Some building centers carry white perf board, which has a melamine coating, and they may even have pegboard panels with decorative photo layers, such as wildlife scenes. Metal pegboard has holes sized to accept regular ¼-inch hangers and accessories, but it generally is stocked only in smaller 16 × 32-inch or 32 × 32-inch panels. Standard pegboard holes are spaced 1-inch apart on-center.

Unless you are hanging your pegboard in a room with open studs, you need to create at least ¾-inch of clearance between the pegboard and the wall so the pins on the hangers have space to be inserted and pivoted. The easiest way to do this is by attaching 1 × 2 furring strips around the perimeter of the pegboard on the back side. For larger pegboard pieces, interim furring strips between the top and bottom rails of the frame will stiffen the project.

Pegboard and pegboard hangers are a timeless storage solution for garages, basements, and workshops that you can adapt easily to other rooms.

Coupled with myriad available hangers, customization can meet your needs precisely. A wealth of pegboard accessories are designed to support shelves, bins, and other storage components that lend themselves well to a home office or craft room. The hooks and hangers designed for use with pegboard have a straight pin and a curved anchor pin that you push through adjoining holes in the pegboard and pivot downward so they hold securely against the back of the pegboard. The holes in most pegboard sold in building centers are nominally ¼-inch in diameter, although their actual size is 9/32 inches so the ¼-inch hangers and hook pins fit into them. Most building centers also carry ⅛-inch hooks, which fit into the less common 3/16-inch holes as well as the standard ¼-inch ones.

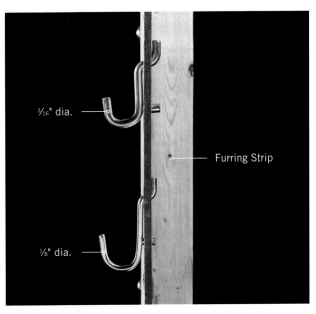

3/16" dia.

Furring Strip

⅛" dia.

The ¼-inch pegboard holes, which are actually 9/32 inches, hold both ¼-inch and ⅛-inch hangers.

TIPS FOR WORKING WITH PEGBOARD

- When cutting a panel, plan your cuts so the distance from the outside holes to the edges of the panels is as uniform as possible.

- Apply a topcoat, such as polyurethane varnish, using a paint roller. This hardens the surface and limits damage around the holes when you insert or remove hooks.

- Create a frame around the back of the panel out of 1 × 2 furring strips to provide clearance space for the hook pins. Conceal the ends of the horizontal strips by running the side strips all the way to the top and bottom edges.

- Apply a bead of construction adhesive before driving 1-inch drywall screws to secure the furring strips (Photo A).

- Build a frame around the furred panel to give it a more finished appearance (Photo B).

Secure the furring strips with construction glue and screws. Add intermediate vertical furring for extra rigidity.

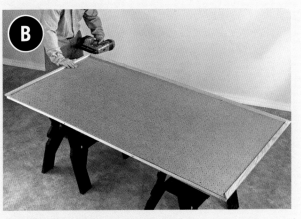

A frame adds a finished appearance that may be more appropriate for a regular living space.

Custom Storage Loft

A storage loft in your garage, basement, or attic gets the clutter out of the way so you can get to work. It doesn't have to be fancy, as this project demonstrates. Although this is a sturdy design, overhead storage is not well-suited for heavy items, so try to limit it to seasonal items and things you can lift easily. This project calls for a plywood floor, but if you are storing items that would benefit from air circulation, you can use wood slats. The storage area as shown is roughly 30 × 30 inches and 6 feet long.

You can adapt the size of this basic utilitarian storage loft bin design to fit your space.

How to Build a Storage Loft

Attach notched joists to the wall cap plates and then screw the outer ledger to the bottom edges of the joist.

Assemble a 2 × 4 frame with the vertical supports attached. Raise the frame and attach it to the top ledger.

Cut platform supports to fit and fasten them inside the frame with screws.

Cut a plywood platform and slide it in place.

TOOLS AND MATERIALS

2 × 4s
Measuring tape
Saw
4-inch screws
Level
Plywood
Nails (optional)
Hammer (optional)

Two walls and the ceiling of a gabled garage support this storage loft, so a pair of 2 × 6 joists attached to the cap plates of the walls run out parallel to the floor. The joist ends are notched to fit underneath the wall cap plates, and are attached to the plates with 4-inch screws driven up through the shoulder of the notch, as well as toenailed into the plate faces. A 75-inch support ledger attaches to the joists 30 inches from the wall (Photo A).

1. Build a rectangular 2 × 4 support frame with outside dimensions equal to the overall project size.

2. Attach 2 × 4 vertical supports to the outer edge of the frame, leaving the ends of the supports open where they will meet the ceiling.

3. With a helper, raise the frame and attach the tops of the vertical supports to the top ledger (Photo B).

4. Make sure the frame is level and screw it to the wall studs with at least two 4-inch screws at each stud, both at the long edge of the frame and the end.

5. Cut 2 × 4 platform supports to fit side-to-side in the frame and install them inside the frame with screws (Photo C).

6. Cut a piece of ¼- or ½-inch plywood for the platform and fit it into the loft (Photo D). You can tack the platform to the frame with small nails if you wish.

Special-Purpose Carts

A DIY rolling trolley like the one in this project offers utility that can be tucked out of sight as needed.

A custom household cart that feels like furniture can expand the utility of any room for any function, and look good in the process. The bar cart, or bar trolley, recently has become an indispensable home aide for many younger homeowners. Printer carts that can live quietly tucked away and rolled into service as needed are popular for storing printers, printing supplies, and other peripherals. Or, when an exercise room reverts into a family room or an entertainment area, simply load a little trolley with snacks and roll it into the room. Workshops, craft rooms, even bedrooms that do double-duty as study areas for home learning are all perfect places to deploy a cart, whether you buy one or build your own custom model.

When designing your own cart, keep the overall height in mind. The cart in this project, for example, is 27-inches tall so you can park it under a table or desktop. Space the shelves at intervals to match the size of the objects you want to transport, such as a printer or your favorite storage bins for crafting supplies. For indoor use, you can keep the wheels or casters relatively small—the one shown here has 3-inch-diameter casters. Today, the popularity of these carts has led to an explosion of wheel and caster styles, many with a very industrial appearance. You can also design a cart for outdoor entertaining or even gardening, in which case you'll want to upgrade to larger wheels that can navigate uneven surfaces.

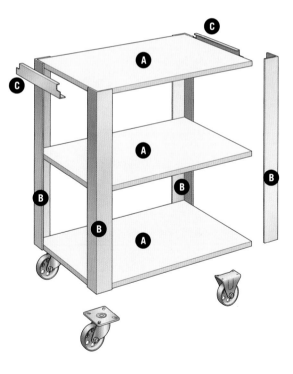

You can adapt this basic bar cart design for just about any purpose or style.

How to Build an Easy House Trolley

TOOLS AND MATERIALS

(1) 1½ × 1½ × 96-inch aluminum angle

Jig saw with metal-cutting blade

Drill

Emery paper or fine file

Sander

Finish of choice

¼ × 1-in. lag screws

#14 × 1 ¼-in. roundhead wood screws

Square

#12 × ¾-in. roundhead wood screws

(1) 5⁄8 × 16 × 72-in. edge-glued pine panel

(2) 1½ × 13-in. cabinet door/drawer pulls

(4) 3-in.-dia. casters (2 swivel, 2 fixed)

CUTLIST

KEY	QTY	PART NAME	DIMENSION	MATERIAL
A	3	Shelf	5⁄8 × 16 × 24"	Pine panel
B	4	Leg	1⁄8 × 1½ × 24"	Aluminum angle
C	2	Pull	1½ × 13"	Metal drawer pull

The three main materials for this project—pine panels, an aluminum angle, and casters—are readily available at any building center. You can redesign the cart using different materials and dimensions, but it's best to include at least three shelves, as they play a structural role in preventing racking.

A

Drill guide holes in the aluminum angle legs for the screws that will attach the shelves.

Attach the finished shelves to the legs.

Attach the fixed casters on one end and the pivoting casters on the other.

1. Cut the legs from the aluminum angle using the jig saw and metal-cutting blade. Such a blade will cut soft metals, as well as harder, ferrous metals.

2. Drill aligned guide holes for the screws that will fasten the legs to the shelves (Photo A). For a light-duty cart such as this, one screw, centered edge to edge, provides adequate support. Make sure to align all screws that will support each shelf in the same plane.

3. Deburr the cut leg ends and remove and rough edges around the holes with emery paper or a fine file.

4. Cut the shelves to size from the pine panel. Sand the ends and surfaces and then apply your finish (it is easier and neater to do this before installation).

5. Lay the top or bottom panel on a flat surface and drill pilot holes through the guide hole and into the panel. Repeat in the appropriate location for each shelf.

6. Attach two of the legs with #14 × 1¼-inch roundhead wood screws.

7. Install the middle shelf and then attach the other pair of legs, squaring the assembly as you go (Photo B).

8. Attach the long drawer pulls to the ends of the top shelf with the gripping flanges facing upward to function as handles.

9. Install the casters with ¾-inch screws (Photo C). Put the swivel casters on one end and the fixed casters on the other.

Adjustable Shelves

An adjustable shelving system adds useful storage capacity to any room, be it a garage workshop, a kitchen or pantry, a home office or closet, and more. These versatile systems are inexpensive and easy to install. They are also simple to remove if your storage needs change.

A basic adjustable system has three parts: the standards, or tracks, that attach to the wall; the shelf brackets that fit into the slots in the tracks; and the shelves. The keys to installation are to securely fasten the tracks at stud locations (avoid using wall anchors) and to align the track slots so the shelves will be level.

The shelf tracks come in a variety of ratings, from slim and lightweight to heavy duty. Most are white or brass, but other colors usually are available, and they can be painted with metal spray paint. Typically, they have pairs of vertical slots that accept the fins on the shelf brackets. The brackets themselves come in various lengths that are designed to support shelves of differing widths. Make sure that the shelf brackets you buy are compatible with your tracks and that they are rated to support the width of your planned shelves.

Because the tracks are sold in a variety of lengths, you can probably install your system without cutting. If you do need to cut them to length, use a hacksaw and make sure you measure from matching ends of each track so the slots will align after cutting. Measure down from the ceiling and mark the height of the track location at each wall stud in the area. If your wall has 16-inch on-center studs, you should be fine installing tracks every 32 inches. If you are a fan of overbuilding, install a track on every stud, but be extra careful to align the slots exactly.

Adjustable metal shelf tracks and support brackets bring handy storage to any room without taking the space over visually.

How to Install Adjustable Shelving

TOOLS AND MATERIALS

Tracks
Brackets
Shelves
Screws
Drill
Level
Chalkline
Hacksaw (optional)
Rubber mallet

1. Install the end tracks first. Center each on the stud and drive screws through the mounting holes in the track, which are usually spaced 12 inches apart.

2. Check plumb by holding a level against the track (Photo A).

3. Snap a chalkline between the two track tops or rest a straight piece of track on the tops as a reference for positioning the intermediate tracks.

4. Install all the remaining tracks.

5. Cut the shelving to length if necessary.

6. Install the shelf brackets in aligned rows by inserting the mounting fin or fins into the track slots (Photo B). Rap them lightly with a rubber mallet to check for a secure set.

7. Rest the shelves on the brackets.

Install the shelf brackets in aligned rows and check that you set them securely.

Screw the vertical tracks to the wall stud locations and check for plumb.

Photo Credits

Zoë Bartholomew
p. 81 (top left)

Rebecca Ittner
p. 106, p. 107, p. 114

Courtesy of Dirk Kinley
p. 115

Larry Okrend
p. 152, p. 154, p. 155, p. 156, p. 157

Ashley McLeod
p. 119 (top right), p. 141 (bottom)

Shutterstock
p. 6, p. 8, p. 12, p. 13., p. 14, p. 15, p. 16., p. 17, p. 18, p. 19, p. 20 (top), p. 21, p. 22, p. 23, p. 24, p. 25, p. 26, p. 27, p. 28, p. 29, p. 30, p. 31, p. 32, p. 33, p. 34, p. 35 (lower left), p. 43, p. 46, p. 47, p. 48 (top and bottom), p. 52 (bottom), p. 54, p. 56, p. 60, p. 62, p. 70, p. 73, p. 81 (top right and bottom), p. 84, p. 85, p. 86, p. 87, p. 88, p. 89 (top), p. 91, p. 96 (top), p. 100, p. 111, (bottom right), p. 112, p. 113, p. 114 (top), p. 116, p. 118, p. 119 (top left), p. 120, p. 128, p. 137 (left), p. 141 (top), p. 142 (top), p. 146, p. 158, p. 159 (top right, bottom left, bottom right), p. 164 (middle)

Metric Conversion Charts

CONVERTING MEASUREMENTS

TO CONVERT:	TO:	MULTIPLY BY:	TO CONVERT:	TO:	MULTIPLY BY:
Inches	Millimeters	25.4	Millimeters	Inches	0.039
Inches	Centimeters	2.54	Centimeters	Inches	0.394
Feet	Meters	0.305	Meters	Feet	3.28
Yards	Meters	0.914	Meters	Yards	1.09
Square inches	Square centimeters	6.45	Square centimeters	Square inches	0.155
Square feet	Square meters	0.093	Square meters	Square feet	10.8
Square yards	Square meters	0.836	Square meters	Square yards	1.2
Cubic inches	Cubic centimeters	16.4	Cubic centimeters	Cubic inches	0.061
Cubic feet	Cubic meters	0.0283	Cubic meters	Cubic feet	35.3
Cubic yards	Cubic meters	0.765	Cubic meters	Cubic yards	1.31
Pounds	Kilograms	0.454	Kilograms	Pounds	2.2

LUMBER DIMENSIONS

NOMINAL - U.S.	ACTUAL - U.S. (IN INCHES)	METRIC	NOMINAL - U.S.	ACTUAL - U.S. (IN INCHES)	METRIC
1 × 2	¾ × 1½	19 × 38 mm	2 × 4	1½ × 3½	38 × 89 mm
1 × 3	¾ × 2½	19 × 64 mm	2 × 6	1½ × 5½	38 × 140 mm
1 × 4	¾ × 3½	19 × 89 mm	2 × 8	1½ × 7¼	38 × 184 mm
1 × 6	¾ × 5½	19 × 140 mm	2 × 10	1½ × 9¼	38 × 235 mm
1 × 8	¾ × 7¼	19 × 184 mm	2 × 12	1½ × 11¼	38 × 286 mm
1 × 10	¾ × 9¼	19 × 235 mm	4 × 4	3½ × 3½	89 × 89 mm
1 × 12	¾ × 11¼	19 × 286 mm	4 × 6	3½ × 5½	89 × 140 mm
2 × 2	1½ × 1½	38 × 38 mm	6 × 6	5½ × 5½	140 × 140 mm
2 × 3	1½ × 2½	38 × 64 mm	8 × 8	7¼ × 7¼	184 × 184 mm

METRIC PLYWOOD

STANDARD SHEATHING GRADE	SANDED GRADE
7.5 mm (⁵⁄₁₆")	6 mm (⁴⁄₁₇")
9.5 mm (⅜")	8 mm (⁵⁄₁₆")
12.5 mm (½")	11 mm (⁷⁄₁₆")
15.5 mm (⅝")	14 mm (⁹⁄₁₆")
18.5 mm (¾")	17 mm (⅔")
20.5 mm (¹³⁄₁₆")	19 mm (¾")
22.5 mm (⅞")	21 mm (¹³⁄₁₆")
25.5 mm (1")	24 mm (¹⁵⁄₁₆")

COUNTERBORE, SHANK & PILOT HOLE DIAMETERS (INCHES)

SCREW SIZE	COUNTERBORE DIAMETER FOR SCREW HEAD	CLEARANCE HOLE FOR SCREW SHANK	PILOT HOLE DIAMETER	
			HARD WOOD	SOFT WOOD
#1	.146 (⁹⁄₆₄)	⁵⁄₆₄	³⁄₆₄	¹⁄₃₂
#2	¼	³⁄₃₂	³⁄₆₄	¹⁄₃₂
#3	¼	⁷⁄₆₄	¹⁄₁₆	³⁄₆₄
#4	¼	⅛	¹⁄₁₆	³⁄₆₄
#5	¼	⅛	⁵⁄₆₄	¹⁄₁₆
#6	⁵⁄₁₆	⁹⁄₆₄	³⁄₃₂	⁵⁄₆₄
#7	⁵⁄₁₆	⁵⁄₃₂	³⁄₃₂	⁵⁄₆₄
#8	⅜	¹¹⁄₆₄	⅛	³⁄₃₂
#9	⅜	¹¹⁄₆₄	⅛	³⁄₃₂
#10	⅜	³⁄₁₆	⅛	⁷⁄₆₄
#11	½	³⁄₁₆	⁵⁄₃₂	⁹⁄₆₄
#12	½	⁷⁄₃₂	⁹⁄₆₄	⅛

Index